Good Essay Writing

SAGE has been part of the global academic community since 1965, supporting high quality research and learning that transforms society and our understanding of individuals, groups, and cultures. SAGE is the independent, innovative, natural home for authors, editors and societies who share our commitment and passion for the social sciences.

Find out more at: **www.sagepublications.com**

Good Essay Writing

A Social Sciences Guide

Fourth Edition

Peter Redman and Wendy Maples

Los Angeles | London | New Delhi
Singapore | Washington DC

First edition published by The Open University 1998
Second edition published 2001. Reprinted 2002, 2003, 2006
Third edition published 2006. Reprinted 2007, 2008, 2009
This fourth edition published 2011

SAGE Publications Ltd
1 Oliver's Yard
55 City Road
London EC1Y1SP

SAGE Publications Inc.
2455 Teller Road
Thousand Oaks, California 91320

SAGE Publications India Pvt Ltd
B1/1 1 Mohan Cooperative Industrial Area
Mathura Road, Post Bag 7
New Delhi 110 044

SAGE Publications Asia-Pacific Pte Ltd
33 Pekin Street #02-01
Far East Square
Singapore 048763

Library of Congress Control Number: 2010936855

British Library Cataloguing in Publication data

A catalogue record for this book is available from the British Library

ISBN 978-0-85702-370-4
ISBN 978-0-85702-371-1 (pbk)

Typeset by C&M Digitals (P) Ltd, Chennai, India
Printed and bound in Great Britain by Ashford Colour Press
Printed on paper from sustainable resources

MIX
Paper from
responsible sources
FSC
www.fsc.org
FSC® C011748

Contents

About the Authors

Peter Redman has been teaching social science at The Open University for the last 20 years. During this time he has worked closely with numerous students helping them reflect on and improve their writing skills. He is a Senior Lecturer in Sociology.

Wendy Maples is a Senior Lecturer in Geography at The Open University. She has been teaching in the Social Sciences for over 20 years. She has worked on a number of interdisciplinary courses, writing course texts in Social Science research methods and Environment, as well as learning development materials for students and teaching development materials for lecturers.

Preface to the Fourth Edition and Acknowledgements

Previous editions of *Good Essay Writing* have aimed to provide practical and easily accessible advice on writing social science essays. The fourth edition continues in this vein but offers, in addition to a completely redesigned and updated text, specifically new material – in particular, critical thinking, reading and literature searches. It also has an accompanying website, accessed at: www.sagepub.co.uk/redman. The Guide and website will be a valuable resource for anyone wishing to reflect on or improve their essay writing skills.

Good Essay Writing is the outcome of a series of collective efforts. Some of the best ideas to be found in the guide came from a team of Open University Associate Lecturers who commented on and contributed to the early drafts of *Good Essay Writing*'s first incarnation. They were Sue Cole, Rosie Collins, Rick Davies, Peter Hull, Mary Larkin, Liz Ockleford, Isobel Shelton and Andy Sutton. Chris Brook, Ross Fergusson, Chris Nichols, Diane Watson and Helen Wescott contributed additional material to the first edition and the second edition incorporated further ideas from Geraldine Carpenter, Vicki Goodwin, Mary Langan, Janet MacDonald and Alison Rolfe. Much of this material reappears in this new edition and our thanks are therefore due to all of these people. Much of the new accompanying website material was developed and written by Rob Parsons, for which many thanks are due. We also owe sincere thanks to Open University Students Evie Beattie; Phil Ellis; Teresa Garrard; Hazel Hart; David Knight; Emma Percy and David Purcell, whose essays were selected to appear in the book or on the website. Special mention should also go to Jonathan Davies, who designed the first edition, and to Peggotty Graham, who supported the original Open University project.

While these contributions proved invaluable, this and previous editions of the guide owe a particular debt of gratitude to two further people. The first is Helen Lentell, who, as Staff Tutor in the Open University in the East Midlands, had the idea for *Good Essay Writing*, put together the original project team and contributed much to the guide's first edition. The second is Lynne Slocombe, who not only edited the first and second editions but also provided much of the material on referencing which reappears here.

Introduction

- How to use this guide
- Will the guide tell you everything about essay writing?

Many students, however experienced, find essay writing difficult. There is, of course, no guaranteed recipe, no absolute method for producing a good essay. However, it is the purpose of this book to recommend and illustrate proven approaches and techniques which, combined with practice, will increase your confidence and skill and thereby improve the quality and effectiveness of your academic writing.

Throughout the book you will find examples of good practice that will help you in this task. These include how to: 'wordstorm' your initial ideas, organize and plan your essay, write effective introductions and conclusions, build an effective argument, use evidence, and provide accurate references. Summary sections help to reinforce your understanding of these issues, while extracts from academic texts and real, sample essays help illustrate the points being made. These all serve to demonstrate how your initial ideas can be transformed into the clear, flowing prose of a well-written essay.

As *Good Essay Writing* has been written by Open University (OU) social sciences staff, you may find terms that are common in the OU but are less common in your home university. For instance, we use the term 'tutor' to describe the person leading teaching on a course – or module – and who is responsible for marking and assessing your essays. In other universities the terms 'lecturer' or 'professor' might be more readily used. You will also find that we focus on the social sciences and use this as a broad generic term which includes subjects such as sociology, politics, geography, psychology, social policy and economics. However, there are many other subject areas where students are required to produce 'social science' essays. For this reason the book and its accompanying website include sample material from business, nursing, environment and education.

In brief, the guide aims to:

- introduce key essay writing skills and accepted conventions in the social sciences;
- recap on social science essay writing skills for those who have already done some studies in the social sciences or related areas;
- introduce more advanced essay writing skills.

If your aim is to write better essays and you want quick, practical advice and guidance that builds on years of successful and high-quality teaching, then *Good Essay Writing* is for you.

1.1   How to use this guide

Inevitably, some readers will be familiar with much of the material in *Good Essay Writing*. However, some aspects may be new to you, and other parts will help you build on or develop what you already know. As such, you should view *Good Essay Writing* as a resource that you can adapt to your own needs.

The chapters that follow cover the main aspects of essay writing, ending with 'Summaries' of some general points to look out for and 'self-test' questions to consolidate your reading.

Chapters 2–6 provide an outline of the characteristics of social science essays; demonstrate some of the essential study skills you will need to prepare for essay writing; explore some basic principles of essay writing; provide recommendations on how to approach different types of essay questions; and discuss planning and preparation.

Chapter 7 looks specifically at forming and shaping an introduction.

Chapter 8 looks at writing the main section of a social science essay, exploring how to structure an argument, how to support your case with evidence, and how to communicate your argument effectively.

Chapter 9 discusses conclusion writing.

Chapter 10 explains how to compile references.

Chapter 11 looks at some common worries that people have about writing essays.

Chapter 12 considers what tutors look for in introductory level, intermediate and advanced essays, and describes common indicators of performance by grade band.

Chapter 13 consists of four examples of full student essays and comments by tutors on the essays' strengths and weaknesses.

Finally, there are two Appendices.

Appendix A lists common editors' notations used by tutors which you may find in feedback on your essays.

Appendix B explains abbreviations and words in foreign languages that are commonly found in English academic writing.

How can you use the guide most effectively?

There are several approaches (as you can see from the bullet points below), and it will probably be best if you try to combine them to produce a strategy that works for you. You might decide to:

- read *Good Essay Writing* from cover to cover;
- skim-read sections that you already know enough about;
- work systematically through individual chapters such as 'Writing the main section';
- concentrate on the Summaries and prompt questions at the end of each chapter;
- use the Contents pages and Index to pinpoint particular issues that are relevant to you and ignore the rest;
- use *Good Essay Writing* as a 'reference' book, returning to it whenever you need to look up something or remind yourself of a particular point;
- use some sections as reference material; for example, the Appendix on common markers' notations.

1.2   Will the guide tell you everything about essay writing?

Good Essay Writing is a quick guide designed to help you build on your essay writing skills and to improve your abilities to communicate effectively as a social scientist. It is not intended to – nor could it – provide all the detailed guidance that you may need for each and every course that you study, nor does it cover more specialized tasks, such as project writing, or how to handle graphs and tables and so on. Similarly, it is not intended as an extended, interactive course in essay writing. Its intention is to be short, practical and easily accessible.

As a result, the guide cannot promise to transform your essay writing over-night. The truth is that there is no magic formula that will guarantee you a good grade for every essay that you produce. In fact, there is no one 'correct' way to write an essay. Sometimes, the most exciting essays will be those that address a question in an unexpected way, that challenge its fundamental premises, or that succeed in producing new insights rather than recycling well-worn ideas. The advice in this guide suggests some generally agreed conventions, but these are not the only ones available and they do not by themselves add up to a great essay.

Your essay writing will improve mainly through your own hard work in thinking things out for yourself, through experience, and through your increasing knowledge of the fields in which you work. The advice you find in *Good Essay Writing* should be used in tandem with the advice you get from your course or module tutor. This advice may be offered in your tutorials or at lectures, or in writing as feedback on your essays. Written feedback can be invaluable, which is why one of the bits of advice offered in *Good Essay Writing* is to read carefully any comments offered by your tutor. You may also have online resources at your university to support study skills, including essay writing. In addition to this, Sage, the co-publishers of this book, have provided a website (www.sagepub.co.uk/redman) that you can access which includes additional materials specifically for use with *Good Essay Writing*. Here you will find a series of activities and downloads, additional sample essays with tutor comments, and a full journal article with guidance on note-taking and referencing. There are also some self-help activities to help you develop good practice and identify areas where you might need further revision. You will find linked activities or downloads on the website when you see this symbol @ in the margin of the text.

'How to . . .' guides like this one are rather like cookery books: they can tell you what the ingredients are, and they can suggest ways to mix the ingredients together. What they cannot do is turn you into a gourmet chef. Like cooking, essay writing is not something you ever stop learning about. However, the advice in *Good Essay Writing* should help you to become more confident and more creative in your work and, in so doing, improve the overall quality of your writing.

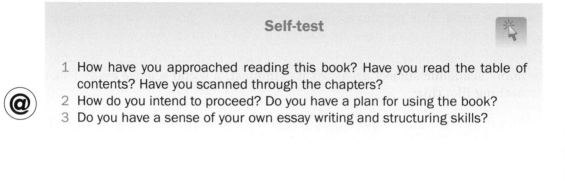

Self-test

1 How have you approached reading this book? Have you read the table of contents? Have you scanned through the chapters?

@

2 How do you intend to proceed? Do you have a plan for using the book?

3 Do you have a sense of your own essay writing and structuring skills?

2

What is a Social Science Essay?

- The structure of a basic social science essay
- What is distinctive about a social science essay?
- Common errors in essays
- Four golden rules for writing a social science essay
- Why an essay is not a report, newspaper article or an exam answer

In this chapter we consider what is distinctive about essay writing and, in particular, essay writing in the social sciences. To start with, we look at the structure of social science essays.

2.1   The structure of a basic social science essay

There are different types of social science essay, and essays of different lengths require slightly different approaches (these will be addressed later). However, all social science essays share a basic structure which is common to many academic subject areas. At its simplest, a social science essay looks something like this:

- Title   Every essay should begin with the title written out in full. In some cases this will simply be the set question or statement for discussion.
- Introduction   The introduction tells the reader what the essay is about.

- Main section   The main section, or 'body', of the essay develops the key points of the argument in a 'logical progression'. It uses evidence from research studies (empirical evidence) and theoretical arguments to support these points.
- Conclusion   The conclusion reassesses the arguments presented in the main section in order to make a final statement in answer to the question.
- List of references   This lists full details of the publications referred to in the text.

2.2 What is distinctive about a social science essay?

As you are no doubt aware, essay writing is a common feature of undergraduate study in many different subjects. What, then, is distinctive about essay writing in the social sciences? There are particular features that characterize social science essays and that relate to what is called the *epistemological* underpinning of work in this area (that is, to ideas about what constitutes valid social scientific knowledge and where this comes from). Among the most important of these characteristics are:

- the requirement that you support arguments with *evidence,* particularly evidence that is the product of systematic and rigorous research (see Sections 6.1 and 8.2);
- the use of *theory* to build explanations about how the social world works (see Section 8.2).

Evidence is important in social scientific writing because it is used to support or query beliefs, propositions or hypotheses about the social world. Let's take an example. A social scientist may ask: 'Does prison work?' This forms an initial *question*, but one that is too vague to explore as it stands. (This question might be about whether prison 'works' for offenders, in terms of providing rehabilitation, or re-education; or it might be about whether it 'works' for victims of crime who may wish to see retribution – or any number of other issues.) To answer the question in mind, the social scientist will need to formulate a more specific *claim,* one that can be systematically and rigorously explored. Such a claim could be formulated in the following terms: 'Imprisonment reduces the likelihood of subsequent reoffending'. This claim can now be subjected to systematic research. In other words, the social scientist will gather *evidence* for and against this claim, evidence that she or he will seek to interpret or *evaluate*. This process of evaluation will tend to support or refute the original claim, but it may be inconclusive, and/or it may generate further questions. Together, these processes of enquiry can be

Figure 1 The circuit of social scientific knowledge

Source: Sherratt et al., 2000, p. 18.

described as forming a 'circuit of social scientific knowledge'. This circuit can be represented as in Figure 1.

Undergraduates may sometimes be asked to conduct their own small-scale research, for instance a small number of interviews, or some content analysis. However, the focus of social science study at undergraduate level, and particularly in the first two years of study, will be largely on the research of others. Generally, in preparing for writing your essays, the expectation will be that you will identify and evaluate evidence from existing research findings. However, the principle holds good: in writing social science essays you will need to find evidence for and against any claim, and you will need to evaluate that evidence.

Theory is important in social scientific writing because the theoretical orientation of the social scientist will tend to inform the types of question she or he asks, the specific claims tested, the ways in which evidence is identified and gathered, and the manner in which this evidence is interpreted and evaluated. In other words, the theoretical orientation of the social scientist is liable to impact upon the forms of knowledge she or he will produce.

Take, for example, the research question we asked above: 'Does prison work?' A pragmatic, policy-oriented social scientist may seek to answer this question by formulating a specific claim of the sort we identified, 'Imprisonment reduces the likelihood of reoffending'. She or he may then gather evidence of reoffending rates among matched groups of convicted criminals, comparing those who were imprisoned with those who were given an alternative punishment such as forms of community service. Evidence that imprisonment did not produce significantly lower rates of reoffending than punishment in the community may then be interpreted as suggesting that prison does not work, or that it works only up to a point. However, another social scientist might look at the same research findings and come to a different conclusion, perhaps

7

that the apparent failure of prison to reduce reoffending demonstrates that its primary purpose lies elsewhere. Indeed, more 'critically' oriented social scientists (for example, those informed by Marxism or the work of Michel Foucault) have sought to argue that the growth of prisons in the nineteenth century was part of wider social attempts to 'discipline', in particular, the working class.

The issue here is not whether these more 'critical' arguments are right or wrong but that a social scientist's theoretical orientation will inform how she or he evaluates the available evidence. In fact, it is likely that a 'critical' social scientist of this sort would even have formulated a different research 'claim'. For example, rather than seeking to test the claim, 'Imprisonment reduces the likelihood of reoffending', the critical social scientist might have sought to test the proposition, 'Prisons are part of wider social strategies that aim to produce "disciplined" subjects'. The point for you to take away from this discussion is, then, that the theories we use shape the forms of social scientific knowledge we produce (see Figure 2).

There is considerable debate within the social sciences about the exact relationship between theory and evidence. To simplify somewhat, some social scientists tend to argue that evidence can be used to support or invalidate the claims investigated by research and thereby produce theoretical accounts of the social world that are more or less accurate. Other social scientists will tend to argue that our theoretical orientations (and the value judgements and taken-for-granted assumptions that they contain) shape the processes of

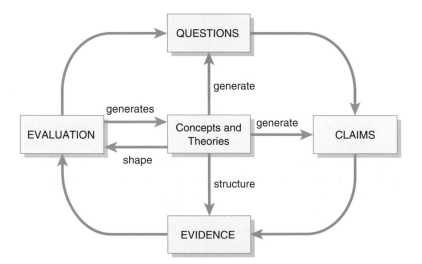

Figure 2 Concepts and theories shape, and are shaped by, the circuit of knowledge

Source: Adapted from Sherratt et al., 2000, p. 18.

social scientific enquiry itself, such that we can never claim to produce a straightforwardly 'accurate' account of the social world. Instead, they suggest that social scientific knowledge is always produced from a particular stand-point and will inevitably reflect its assumptions.

Some of the implications of these points are discussed further in Sections 6.2 and 8.2. For now, what you need to grasp is that essay writing in the social sciences is distinguished by its emphasis on: the use of researched evidence to support arguments and on theory as central to the process by which we build accounts of social worlds. Your own writing will need to engage with both elements.

2.3   Common errors in essays

Having identified what distinguishes a social science essay we can return to the more practical task of how to write one. This process is elaborated in the chapters that follow, but before getting into the details of this, we should think about what commonly goes wrong in essay writing.

Perhaps the most common mistakes in essay writing, all of which can have an impact on your marks, are:

- failure to answer the question;
- failure to write using your own words;
- poor use of social scientific skills (such as handling theory and evidence);
- poor structure;
- poor grammar, punctuation and spelling; and
- failure to observe the word limit (where this is specified).

Failing to answer the question sounds easy enough to avoid, but you might be surprised how easy it is to write a good answer to the wrong question. Most obviously, there is always the risk of misreading the question (suggestions on how to avoid this can be found in Section 4.1). However, it is frequently the case that questions will 'index' a wider debate and will want you to review and engage with this. Thus, you need to avoid the danger of understanding the question but failing to connect it to the debate and the body of literature to which the question refers (this point is discussed more fully in Sections 5.3 and 8.1). Equally, particularly on more advanced undergraduate courses, you are likely to be asked to work from an increasing range of sources. The dangers here include failing to select the *most* relevant material and failing to organize the material you have selected in a way that best fits the question. Therefore, make sure that you take time to read the question properly to ensure that you understand what is being asked. Next, think carefully about whether there is a debate that 'lies behind' the question. Then be sure to identify the material that addresses the question most fully.

Writing in your own words is crucial because this is the best way in which you can come to understand a topic, and the only way of demonstrating this understanding to your tutor. How to avoid 'plagiarism' (or copying what someone else has already written or said) is dealt with in detail in Section 11.5. The important point to remember is that if you do plagiarize, your essay risks receiving a fail grade, and if you plagiarize repeatedly you risk further sanctions. You must therefore always put arguments in your own words except when you are quoting someone directly (in which case you must use the appropriate referencing conventions, discussed in Chapter 10). One positive side of what might seem like a draconian rule is that you will remember better what you have put in your own words. This ensures that you will have the fullest possible understanding of your course. If there is an end-of-course exam, such an understanding will be a real asset.

Social science essays also need to demonstrate an effective use of social scientific skills. Perhaps the most obvious of these skills is the ability to deploy theory and evidence in an appropriate manner (as you saw in the previous section, this is what distinguishes social scientific essay writing). However, particularly as you move on to more advanced undergraduate courses, you should also keep in mind the need to demonstrate such things as confidence in handling social scientific concepts and vocabulary; an awareness of major debates, approaches and figures in your field; the ability to evaluate competing arguments; and an awareness of potential uncertainty, ambiguity and the limits of knowledge in your subject. These are important because they indicate your ability to work creatively with the tools of the social scientist's trade (these issues are addressed throughout the following chapters).

An effective structure is important and pragmatic because it helps the person who marks your essay to understand what is going on. By contrast, a list of unconnected ideas and examples is likely to confuse, and will certainly fail to impress. The simplest way to avoid this is to follow the kind of essay writing conventions briefly outlined above and discussed in later chapters of this guide. Chapter 8, on the main body of the essay, is particularly relevant here, but you will also need to keep in mind the importance of a well-written introduction and conclusion to an effectively structured argument (see Chapters 7 and 9).

The ability to spell, punctuate and use grammar correctly is, generally speaking, something you are expected to have mastered prior to embarking on a degree-level course. As sections 8.4 and 11.4 explain, this is really a matter of effective communication. While it is the content of your essay that will win you the most marks, you need to be able spell, punctuate and use grammar effectively in order to communicate what you have to say. Major problems in this area will inevitably hold down your marks, so if this is an issue in your work, it will be a good idea to seek further help.

Finally, observing the word limit is important – and, as you probably realize, more difficult than it sounds. Further advice on this matter is available in Section 11.1, but the simplest advice is always to check whether there is a word limit and what this is, and then to be ruthless with yourself, focusing only on the material that is most pertinent to the question. If you find that you have written more words than is allowed, you will need to check for irrelevant discussions, examples, or even wordy sentence construction. Too few words may indicate that you haven't provided the depth of discussion required, or that you have omitted essential points or evidence.

In the light of the above, we can identify four golden rules for effective social scientific essay writing.

2.4   Four golden rules for writing a social science essay

Rule 1:   Answer the question that is asked.
Rule 2:   Write your answer in your own words.
Rule 3:   Think about the content of your essay, being sure to demonstrate good social scientific skills.
Rule 4:   Think about the structure of your essay, being sure to demonstrate good writing skills, and observing any word limit.

2.5   Why an essay is not a report, newspaper article or an exam answer

This section has mainly focused on what is distinctive about a social science essay, but there is something distinctive about essays in general that is worth keeping in mind. Many students come from professional backgrounds where report writing is a common form of communication. For other students a main source of information is newspapers or websites. These are all legitimate forms of writing that serve useful purposes – but, apart from some of the content on academic websites, they just aren't essays. There are exam conventions that make exam writing – even 'essay style' exams – different from essay writing.

In part, this is to do with 'academic register' or 'voice'. Part of what you will develop as you become a stronger essay writer is a 'voice' that is your own, but that conforms to the conventions of academic practice. For social scientists, as we have noted above, this practice includes the use of evidence to support an argument and providing references that show where your ideas and evidence have come from. It also includes the ability to write with some confidence, using the vernacular – or language – of your subject area. Different forms of writing serve different purposes. The main purpose of academic writing is to develop and share knowledge and understanding. In some academic journals this can take the form of boisterous debate, with different academics fully and carefully defending, or arguing for, one position or another. For students of social science, however, there may be less at stake, but essays should nevertheless demonstrate knowledge and understanding of a particular issue or area. Conforming to some basic conventions around how to present ideas and arguments, helps us more easily to compare those ideas, just as conforming to the rules of a game makes it easier for one sports team to play against another: if one team is playing cricket and the other baseball, we will find there are similarities (both use bats, have innings, make runs), but there will also be lots of awkward differences. In the end, neither the players nor the spectators are likely to find it a very edifying experience. The following looks at other forms of serious writing that you may be familiar with, but that just aren't cricket.

Report writing

Reports take a variety of forms, but typically involve: an up-front 'executive summary', a series of discussions, usually with numbered headings and subheadings. They are also likely to include 'bullet points' that capture an idea or argument in a succinct way. Professional reports may include evidence, arguments, recommendations and references. You may already have spotted some of the similarities with essays – and the crucial differences. Let's begin with the similarities. Reports and essays both involve discussion, the use of evidence to support (or refute) a claim or argument, and a list of references. Both will have an introductory section, a main body and a conclusion. However, the differences are important. With the exception of very long essays (dissertations and the like), essays do not generally have numbered headings and subheadings. Nor do they have bullet points. They also don't have executive summaries. And, with some notable exceptions (such as essays around areas of social policy perhaps), social science essays don't usually require you to produce policy recommendations. The differences are significant, and are as much about style as they are about substance.

Journalistic writing

For many students, journalistic styles of writing are most familiar. Catchy headlines (or 'titles') are appealing, and newspapers' to-the-point presentation may make for easier reading. News stories, however, follow a different set of requirements to essays – a different set of 'golden rules'. In general, newspaper and website news articles foreground the 'who, what, where, when and why' of a story in the first paragraph. The most important information is despatched immediately, with the assumption that all readers will read the headline, most readers will read the first paragraph, and dwindling numbers will read the remainder of the article. Everyday newspaper articles often finish with a 'whimper' for this reason, and there may be no attempt to summarize findings or provide a conclusion at the end – that's not the role of news journalists. (Though there is quite a different set of rules for 'Op Ed' or opinion pieces.) Student essays, by contrast, should be structured to be read from beginning to end. The introduction should serve to 'outline' or 'signpost' the main body of the essay, rather than cover everything in one fell swoop; the main body should proceed with a clear, coherent and logical argument that builds throughout; and the essay should end with a conclusion that ties the essay together.

Exam writing

Again, exam writing has similarities and differences with essay writing. Perhaps the main differences are these: under exam conditions, it is understood that you are writing at speed and that you may not communicate as effectively as in a planned essay; you will generally not be expected to provide references (though you may be expected to link clearly authors and ideas). Longer exam answers will need to include a short introduction and a conclusion, while short answers may omit these. Indeed, very short answers may not resemble essays at all as they may focus on factual knowledge or very brief points of comparison.

Summary

- A basic social science essay has the following: a title, an introduction, a main section, a conclusion, and a list of references.
- Essays in the social sciences are distinguished by their emphasis on the use of evidence to evaluate arguments and the use of theory to build accounts of the social world.
- There is some debate in the social sciences on the relationship between theory and evidence.

(Continued)

(Continued)

- There are four golden rules of social science essay writing:

  1 Answer the question that is asked.
  2 Write your answer in your own words.
  3 Think about the content of your essay, being sure to demonstrate good social scientific skills.
  4 Think about the structure of your essay, being sure to demonstrate good writing skills.

- Social science essay writing is distinctive from other forms of serious writing such as reports, newspaper articles and exams. Essay writing is distinctive both in terms of its style as well as its substance.

Self-test

1 What are the two most important characteristics of social science writing?
2 What are the components of the circuit of knowledge? How does the circuit help us understand social science essays?
3 What are the most common errors markers see in social science essays?
4 What are the four 'golden rules'?
5 What distinguishes a social science essay from a newspaper article; a report; an exam answer?

3

Stages of Writing, from Preparation to Final Version

- Read the question and any guidance notes
- Use feedback
- Identify and organize the relevant material
- First draft to final version
- Time management

Here are some reminders for those of you already experienced in essay planning, and some suggestions for anyone coming to social science essay writing for the first time. In short, there are seven stages to writing an essay:

1 Reading and understanding the question
2 Identifying the relevant material
3 Making an essay plan
4 Writing a first draft
5 Reviewing the first draft and writing a second draft
6 Double-checking the administrative requirements of the essay
7 Writing a final version.

In this chapter, we will take an overview of these stages. In addition, we look at some other aspects of planning that you will encounter before you put pen to paper. Thorough preparation and planning is the basis of any good piece of written work, and it really is worth putting some effort into it.

3.1   Read the question and any guidance notes

The best advice anyone can offer you when you embark on an essay is to *read the question*. As you will see in Chapter 4, you need to spend time 'unpacking' the question and being certain you understand both what the content, or main topics or issues, of the essay should be, and how you are expected to address this (as indicated by the 'command' or 'process' words and type of question). Here we will consider the importance of this seemingly simple practice, and of considering any guidance notes you've been given, either as part of the essay question, or in the form of feedback on a previous essay.

Essay guidance notes

In many universities, in addition to the question itself, you will be given guidance on how to answer the question. This may take the form of formally written notes, or it might be verbal instructions from your tutor. In either case, be certain you are clear about this guidance as there may be suggestions about source material, or caveats about areas that are precluded. Introductory level courses may also include guidance about how to structure your essay which you should follow to the letter.

Let's look at an example:

Outline the role of risk in contemporary society and the idea that we live in a risk society. Your essay should aim to show the role of the social sciences in understanding risks and how people live with them.

In this assignment, you are asked to produce a descriptive essay that considers the role of risk in contemporary society. You are asked to consider Beck's argument that we live in a 'risk society' and to provide relevant examples, illustrations or case studies in support of this. You will need to utilize different forms of evidence to help you examine Beck's ideas. On this module, we have considered, for instance: the everyday ways of dealing with risks, the notion that defining risks depends on the complex and contested production of knowledge, the ways in which people perceive and act in relation to knowledge about risks, the role of experts in making risks known to the lay public, and the ways in which people live with and respond to expert ideas about risk. Remember to reference your sources in the body of the essay and to provide a list of references at the end of your essay.

Word count: 1,250.

(Adapted from DD101 'Introducing the Social Sciences', 2009J, Assignment Booklet 2, The Open University.)

This example is taken from a Level I, or freshman year, module and the guidance is fairly specific. The students are told that they are producing a descriptive essay that outlines 'risk' and Ulrich Beck's argument that we live in a 'risk society' in particular. The second part of the question asks students to consider the kind of social science evidence that might be drawn upon in arguing that we live in a risk society, and gives examples of how this has been addressed on the module. However, the guidance also tells students to find case studies and other illustrative material – but which case studies or other examples is left to the students to decide for themselves.

There is also an implicit suggested structure to the essay. Can you make it out? First, students are asked to outline the idea of risk, and to describe what Ulrich Beck means by 'risk society' – to demonstrate their understanding of his argument. Second, students are asked to look at various bits of illustrative material, case studies or social scientific evidence to demonstrate a) what Beck means, and b) how people 'live with' risk. Third, students are asked to think about what social science brings to an understanding of 'risk' and the 'risk society' – this could involve looking at the 'circuit of knowledge' (see Section 2.2) and showing how social scientists approach both ideas and evidence.

Finally, as you see above, guidance normally includes a word count. Your module or university will have guidelines on how much latitude there is in keeping to the word count. In many social science departments, you will find you are expected to keep to the word count, give or take 5 or 10 per cent. So, a 1,000 word essay could be between 950 and 1,050 or between 900 and 1,100 words long and still meet the word count requirement.

Feedback or individual guidance

Preparing to write your essay should begin with your previous piece of work. Take a look at the box below.

What to do when your essay comes back

Maggie Coats

Maggie Coats is an Associate Lecturer at the Open University. These are her suggestions for learning from your last essay.

If you're like most other people, when you get an essay back you'll check the grade first, read any general comments from your tutor and quickly flip through

(Continued)

(Continued)

the rest looking for any major embarrassments. You'll probably read it with more care only if the tutor has written something particularly complimentary or irritating. However, learning from previous pieces of writing is an important way of building on your writing skills.

- Take a quick look at the score and any general comments. Feel pleased, angry or despairing, depending on your grade/mood, then put the essay aside until you are ready to look at it with a more 'objective' eye.
- Give yourself 20 to 30 minutes to look over the essay in detail.
- Reread any general comments and note the main points.
- Reread the essay itself, including any more specific comments made by your tutor; mark your responses to these comments. Do you agree or disagree? Is there anything you don't understand?
- Next, reread your tutor's general comments. Can you see what the tutor is saying?
- On a separate sheet, write down one or two key points that will improve your performance when writing the next assignment. File these.

Source: Adapted from Coats, undated, Handout Material 2.

If you have reflected on previous work in this manner, you will be in a better position to tackle the essay in hand.

What to do if you don't get feedback, or feedback is minimal

At some universities, it is common not to get much in the way of individual feedback on your work. In this case, you may need to be a bit more industrious in figuring out what to do to improve your next assignment. Sometimes tutors will offer generic feedback to the whole class – things that most people did well or poorly. If this is the case, read through your essay, and look at your essay plan (see below) and try to see where your own work has followed the good practice identified by your tutor and, likewise, where it hasn't met your tutor's expectations. You can also use this book as a 'check' on your work. Of course you won't be able to use it to identify your understanding of subject content, but you can use it to help you check whether you have read the question and followed its 'commands' (Section 4.1). Upcoming chapters will help you to identify whether you have written a useful introduction, a coherent main body, a convincing conclusion and an accurate list of references (Chapters 7–10).

As Maggie Coats suggests, try to be objective when looking over your work – the idea is to learn from your previous work, so that you can improve on your next essay.

3.2   Identify and organize the relevant material: drafting an essay plan

Once you have a clear idea of what the question is asking, and particular areas you need to concentrate on improving, your next task is to identify and organize the material you will be using in your essay. We will look at researching and note-taking for essay writing in more detail in Chapter 5, and Chapters 7–10 look at the essential components of an essay. Here we offer a quick overview of some of the main activities you will need to do:

- Read through any existing notes that you have, from lectures, seminars or texts; read or reread the book chapters or journal articles specified for this particular essay; and advanced search recommended or linked academic websites. Make notes about all relevant material.
- Keep careful and detailed notes of sources for your reference list (see Chapters 5 and 10).

Having identified the relevant material, you will need to organize this into a shape that addresses the question. Here are some suggestions for tackling this task.

- 'Wordstorm' your ideas for the essay (that is, jot down a list of questions and issues prompted by the question, all the relevant examples you can think of, and any other related evidence). For many people, this is most productively done with pen and paper, but if you wordprocess your notes you might like to use wordstorming software, like Wordle (www.wordle.net). This kind of software can help you see graphically where you have lots of material or ideas, and where your notes are lacking. To see a Wordle of this chapter, see Figure 3.
- Re-check your notes and add left-out material (do another search).
- Then link and order connected ideas and points. One way to do this is to draw a 'mindmap' of points relevant to the question. This is a bit like wordstorming but adopts a diagrammatic form. Mindmapping is very good for making strong visual links between different parts of an argument. Most people find mindmapping easiest using pen and paper, but there are increasing numbers of software packages that help with mindmapping notes, such as Compendium or OneNote. (Figure 4 shows an example of a mindmap used to prepare for writing 'Essay 1' which appears in Chapter 13.)

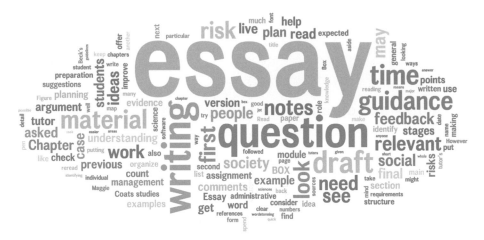

Figure 3 A Wordle of this chapter

- Write out points, examples, ideas and connected theories on separate sheets of paper, 'post-its', or index cards. Group and re-group these until you've got them in a logical order (Section 8.1 offers ideas for creating a 'logical progression' in your argument). Write this out as a list, using numbers and sub-numbers or bullet points. This is a 'linear' essay plan for the main body of the essay (you can worry about the introduction and conclusion later).
- Ideas may come to you at unexpected moments – for these keep a notebook handy and jot them down.

You will see from the plans above that there is a familiar 'shape' to the essay. There is always an introduction and a conclusion (and a reference list), and the main body of the essay focuses on three main points. One of the skills you will develop as you write is selectivity. It is important not to write 'everything' you know about a subject, but to pick out the most essential points. Sometimes the essay question itself will indicate the most important areas to cover, and sometimes this will be suggested in any guidance notes. Sometimes, however, you will need to decide this for yourself. There are a number of tricks to this. The first is to look at your mindmap or linear notes and decide which points your essay can do without – which points will make little difference to an understanding of the topic. The second is to identify the most important point – the issue or idea on which all other points hinge. The third is to ask the 'so what?' question. Put simply, if another student were to ask you 'so what?' about a key point you have identified, would you be able to answer? If not, either this point is less important to the essay – or you need to do some more reading and consolidating of your thoughts.

Stages of writing, from preparation to final version:

Figure 4 Example of a mindmap of Essay 1 in Chapter 13: *'School is a significant site in which sex/gender is produced.'* Discuss.

'School is a significant site in which sex/gender is produced.' Discuss.

Introduction (write this last)

Main body

1 Social constructivism v. biological reductivism (Weedon, 1999; Foucault, 1977, 1984; Lacquer, 1990; Butler, 1993, 2004). Hard and 'soft' social constructivism, e.g. issue of social agency (Butler, 1993 v. Connell, 1995).
2 The active production of sex/gender in schools: recent literature

   a Thorne (1993) US elementary schools and teachers' talk
   b Epstein and Johnson (1994) pupils' clothes
   c Students as active agents, e.g. handball (Thorne, 1993), also mistletoe (Kehily and Nayak, 1996)
   d Negotiating the curriculum and differentiated masculinities (Connell, 1993 and Mac an Ghaill, 1994)

3 Sex and gender and other subjectivities: masculinity/femininity and age, class, ethnicity, sexuality

   a Epstein and Johnson (1998) 'intra-ethnic identification' (find quote about Shamira being a 'tart'?)
   b Mac an Ghaill (1994) boys' sexualized talk
   c Hmm – no room for age – class will be covered a bit with Mac an Ghaill
   d Need to include POWER and wider social relations

Conclusion – review evidence, modification of social constructionist account, and note relation between sex/gender and other subject positions, restate claim.

Figure 5 An example of a linear essay plan relating to Essay 1 in Chapter 13

3.3 Drafting stages

We will look at the elements involved in structuring an essay in more detail in Chapter 8, but here is an outline of the stages that lead from first draft to final product:

- Write out the question at the beginning of your first draft so that you keep its exact wording in front of you to ensure you are answering the question that is asked.
- Working from your essay plan, begin writing a first draft. Do the best you can, but see it as a first draft and expect to make some improvements – you may need to revise your plan as the essay takes shape. Don't worry, this is perfectly normal!
- Once your first draft has some shape, you may need to go back to your notes to check your references and you may want to move sentences, or even paragraphs, around. Your second draft may deviate from your original plan – this

is fine, as long as what you have written makes sense (proceeds in a logical fashion).

- If you have time, it is helpful to put the essay aside for at least a day to let the dust settle, show it to a friend or another student to get feedback, and then reread the question and the essay yourself. Its strengths and weaknesses should now be a lot clearer to you.
- You're now in a position to write your definitive answer, and this is the time to consider more carefully your presentation (sentence structure, grammar, etc.) and to check for clarity of expression. It is good practice to 'spell check' your work, but remember the limits of spell check – you still need to re-read your work to be sure it actually makes sense. Learn the difference between there, their and they're and where the possessive apostrophe goes, depending on whether a word is singular, plural or ends in an 's'.
- Double-check any administrative requirements: have you completed your references in the required format; is the essay double-spaced and in the right sized font (some tutors specifically ask for 12 point font so the essay is easier to read); have you put page numbers on each page; is your name and/or student number at the top of each sheet?

Check through any assignment guidelines, and be sure you have followed any administrative guidance:

- ☐ Is there a recommended format for the header – for instance, should you include your name or student number, the module title, tutor's name, date of submission, etc.?
- ☐ Are you expected to have a title page – what should be included?
- ☐ What is expected in the footer? Page numbers? Anything else?
- ☐ Is there a specified font or typeface, and should the essay be double-spaced? Is there a margin requirement?
- ☐ When and where is the assignment DUE? Is there a cut-off time, as well as a date? Is there a specific location, email or drop box?

- When this is complete, submit the essay – and wait for feedback with quiet confidence.

3.4 Time management

As the previous sections in this chapter have begun to suggest, as you move from your initial preparation to writing your final draft, you will need to plan your time carefully. Effective time management involves being realistic. You will obviously want to set aside as much time as possible for your essay. However, other important commitments may mean that you need to structure the time available with care. As early as possible, look in your diary and, working backwards from your submission date, identify when you are going to be able to do the work. Next, prioritize your tasks and allocate your time accordingly. For example, if you are clear about the question from the start, you will probably have to spend less time on research. If you spend adequate time planning your essay, you may well find that writing the first draft is much easier. As you move through your tasks, concentrate on achieving your major goals. For example, when reading for the essay, don't get distracted by material that is interesting but less relevant to the essay question. Similarly, when writing your draft, try not to get bogged down crafting perfect sentences or clarifying a single point. Focus on putting the whole argument in place and then go back to rework individual sections and improve your style. Good time management will not necessarily mean that producing an essay is free from stress, but it will allow you to make the most of your circumstances.

The following chapters of this guide offer more detailed help through the process of essay preparation and planning, and of first draft to final version – in short, putting together a social sciences essay.

Summary

- Make use of sources of guidance.
- Essay writing has seven principal stages:

  1 Reading and understanding the question
  2 Identifying the relevant material
  3 Making an essay plan
  4 Writing a first draft
  5 Reviewing the first draft and writing a second draft
  6 Double-checking the administrative requirements of the essay
  7 Writing a final version.

- Realistic time management is central to effective essay writing.

Self-test

1 What are the seven stages of writing an essay?
2 How can you use guidance notes – notes for the essay and notes on your previous work? How can these integrate with the guidance on offer in this book?
3 How do you prefer to organize your essay plan – with a mindmap? – using linear notes? Have you tried out any planning software that might help you represent your thoughts?
4 How can you ensure you include the most important material in your essay plan?
5 How can you ensure you have enough time to complete your essay by the cut-off date?

4

Matching the Answer to the Question

- Unpacking the question
- 'Process' and 'content' words
- Cognitive skills
- Answering advocacy questions
- Answering compare and contrast questions
- Answering evaluation questions

Social science questions are often composed of two parts: the topic, issue, idea or position you are expected to consider, and the action or process you are required to do. These processes require different cognitive skills at different levels – from the ability to describe to the ability to analyse and evaluate. In addition, many social science essay questions ask you to consider one or more critical positions or arguments that you are then required to advocate, compare and contrast, or evaluate, which at different levels of study can mean different things. 'Unpacking the question' can be a tricky business, but below we offer guidance on how to simplify the process and accurately match your answer to the question asked.

4.1   Reading the question

As noted in Chapter 2, one common mistake students make is not answering the question that is set. In order to avoid this, a primary task is to read the question carefully and to 'unpack' its instructions. As we showed in Chapter 3, this may include reading carefully any additional guidance and following that to the letter. In addition, however, you will need to unpack the question itself. In so doing you should:

* Identify the 'content' words. These tell you what topics, issues and/or concepts you will be writing about.
* Identify the 'command', or 'process' words (for example, 'discuss', 'evaluate', 'explore'). These tell you *how* you should answer the question. Identifying the process words is just as important as identifying the content words, as we will demonstrate below.

Let's consider the question:

'The family in Britain is in crisis.' Discuss.

'Family', 'Britain', and 'crisis' are the content words. So, the evidence, concepts, theories and claims that you need to explore should focus on whether there is a crisis in the family in Britain and what 'crisis' might mean in this context. Depending on the social sciences subject you are studying, there may be an emphasis on historical changes in the family structure, so part of your evidence could include a comparison of the family in different eras. Or, your module may have emphasized an international approach, in which case some comparison with other nations might be relevant. We will consider more examples of essay questions later, so you can get more of a feel for how the context of your subject will inflect your essays.

'Discuss' is the command word (implying that you have to explore the evidence for and against the statement).

4.2 Command words and cognitive skills

Although there is not a strict progression of cognitive skills in the social sciences you will probably find that you are asked for more description (knowledge) in the early stages of your studies, and more evaluation (understanding) in the later stages. Also, as you progress, it will be expected that the descriptions you *are* asked to produce will be more detailed, complex or subtle. Evaluations may involve more variables, or more difficult issues. In broad terms, you will be demonstrating greater knowledge and increasingly complex understanding in your intermediate and advanced essays.

The following box provides a list and explanation of common command words, organized in terms of the general cognitive skill being tested.

Command or process words in essay questions

- **Description**

To describe something is to provide an account, in your own words or through an illustration, that tells the reader that you know what something is and can depict its main features. To describe a television show, you might indicate its genre, notable characters, 'stars', intended audience, audience figures, and indicate some aspects of the storyline, main topics or issues. For instance: '*The Wire* is an hour-long drama series featuring drug dealers in Baltimore. The characters are well-realized and complex, with a number of the actors having previously lived in the area. The audience for *The Wire* is not dissimilar to that for other adult drama series such as *Hill Street Blues* or *The Sopranos*. *The Wire* is distinctive, though, in part due to its uncompromising use of the Baltimore vernacular – a difficult to understand dialect. Despite this, the programme won critical praise and high viewing figures.'

Process words:

Describe	Give an (detailed) account of . . .
Define	State the exact meaning of a word or phrase. In some cases it may be necessary or desirable to examine different possible or often used definitions.
Depict	Show.
Identify	Find and describe an example or issue.
Illustrate	Make clear and explicit. Usually requires the use of carefully chosen examples.
State	Present in a brief, clear way.
What is/are . . .	Identify and describe.

- **Summary**

Writing an effective summary demonstrates knowledge of information and/or ideas. The skill here is to distil information or ideas, often into a very few words. You may find that summary-type questions will benefit from graphics or tables as part of your answer. To summarize a journal article, you would give the author, date and title of the publication (as in a reference), indicate the article's key points, the main examples offered, and the author's conclusion. At a more advanced level, you might situate the article in its academic subject context, indicating if it is responding to or part of a particular debate or tradition of thought. It is also common to be asked to summarize the content of, for instance, a policy document as part of a wider essay question.

Process words:

Outline	Give the main features or general principles of a subject, omitting minor details and emphasizing structure and arrangement.

Summarize	Give a concise, clear account of a subject, presenting the chief factors and omitting minor details and examples.
What are the main features of . . .	Select the more significant features (of an issue, project, etc.) and present them coherently.

- **Interpretation**

This moves you beyond description to developing understanding, for instance, by suggesting connections between features. For instance: 'Compare Bauman's and Veblen's perspectives on consumption'. This question suggests that there are (at least) two competing theories that can help to explain consumption. At a basic level, there is some description, or summary, necessary to answer this question: you would need to summarize both Bauman's and Veblen's theories in order to compare them. However, there is also some interpretation or 'sense-making' required. Particularly at a higher level, you would need to consider how it is that Veblen and Bauman arrive at different positions – what are the social contexts of their writing? This might include some mention of the different time periods in which they were writing (Veblen – late 1800s; Bauman – late 1900s), and other different social contexts.

Process words:

Compare	Look for similarities and differences between, and, at more advanced levels, reach conclusions about which is preferable and justify this clearly (see *Evaluation*).
Compare and contrast	Find some points of common ground between *x* and *y* and show where or how they differ.
Contrast	Set in opposition in order to bring out the differences sharply.
Distinguish or differentiate between . . .	Show differences between . . .

- **Discussion**

As in ordinary life, a discussion involves recognizing two or more positions in relation to a topic or question, how they differ from each other, and how valid or effective an account each offers. A public debate, with proposers and seconders, is one kind of discussion, but others may be less formally structured. Discussions may be at different levels – from more descriptive accounts of different positions, through to critical, evaluative accounts that identify the value basis and strengths and weaknesses of different positions. Unlike ordinary pub-type discussion, academic discussion should develop an argument in a logical and coherent fashion and reach a conclusion. 'Discuss' questions may be the

(Continued)

(Continued)

most common questions you will come across in social science. The word 'discuss' often follows a provocative or contentious statement, for instance: '"Strong leaders are an inevitable and necessary part of representative democracy." Discuss.' In this case, there is a claim offered in the question's quotation – it is up to you to discuss the merits or otherwise of the claim by looking at the evidence and logic of the claim and any attendant argument (or theories on which the claim is based). Note that you are not asked definitively to agree or disagree: you may find convincing points on both sides of the debate, or you might, at the higher levels of study in particular, take issue with the basis of the question, perhaps by interrogating what is meant by 'leaders' or even 'representative democracy'.

Process words:

Consider	Look at two (or more) sides of an argument, and present the logic, evidence, etc. of both sides.
Debate	Set up a claim or argument, presenting evidence for and against.
Discuss	Present two (or more) sides of an issue or argument and any implications.
What arguments can be made for and against the view that . . .	Look at both sides of an argument.

- **Explanation**

This deepens understanding by identifying causes. Often 'explain'-type questions are attached to historical shifts or changes. 'Explain' questions can also be used to set up an exploration of issues around difference. For instance, 'Account for the difference in wages between men and women in the USA, before and after the Equal Pay Act (1963)'. The task here is two-fold: to discuss that there are differences in wages, and then to explain the socio-historical contexts that led to pay disparity and the different socio-historical (and employment) contexts that maintain (a lesser) disparity. At the higher levels, you might raise related questions, such as other socio-demographic variables that lead to differences in pay: age, race, ethnicity, etc.

Process words:

Account for	Explain, clarify, give reasons for.
Explain	Give details about how and why it is so.
How/Why is it . . .	Give an explanation, including the reasons for or cause of.

- **Evaluation**

This requires understanding that is genuinely critical and involves either testing the strengths and weaknesses of an explanation or considering the degree of success of an action, policy or argument. The former can be achieved by comparing the explanation to particular cases or examples and asking whether the argument can in fact be backed up by evidence. In the latter case, evaluation asks you to judge the effectiveness of a policy or action by looking for cases where the action has been worthwhile or successful and also for cases where things have not worked out – and to provide a balanced, but critical, analysis of this. Similar skills are involved in both instances: you are effectively making an argument on the pros and cons of a particular view or approach – weighing them up, in light of the coherence of the argument, or the strength of the evidence. A more 'evaluative' version of the equal pay question above might look something like this: 'Evaluate the claim that the Equal Pay Act of 1963 has made little or no difference to the wages of women in the workplace.' Here the task is to evaluate the claim that the Equal Pay Act was useless. This rendering of the question will require (at least) two lines of enquiry: that on the one hand there have been other reasons why women's pay has improved and, on the other, that, despite legislation, unequal pay remains a significant issue. In order to explore these, you would need to find evidence, probably at least partly in the form of statistics, to demonstrate both change – and stasis – and theories that explain why federal legislation has been helpful/unhelpful in promoting social and economic change.

Process words:

Assess	Determine the value of, weigh up.
Criticize	Make a judgement (backed by a discussion of the evidence or reasoning involved) about the merit of theories or opinions or about the facts of a matter.
Evaluate	Make an appraisal of the worth/validity/effectiveness of something in the light of its accuracy or usefulness.
How far . . . /To what extent . . .	Usually involves looking at evidence/arguments – for and against – and weighing them up.
Justify	Show adequate grounds for decisions or conclusions, answer the main objections likely to be made about them.

- **Other common process words**

Other words that you are likely to see in essay questions include:

Analyze	Resolve into its component parts. Examine critically or minutely. 'Analyze' may be used as a descriptive command word at the higher levels of study, or it might be used to indicate an 'evaluate' requirement.
Examine the . . .	Look in detail at this line of argument.

(Continued)

(Continued)

You may also find that many questions are composites – 'Evaluate the claim that . . . Illustrate your answer with . . . '; 'Give an example of . . . Explain, using Marx or Weber, how . . . '

(*Source:* Adapted from Sue Cole, Associate Lecturer, and Pauline Harris, Assistant Staff Tutor (undated), 'Handout Material 2', and Phil Sarre, Senior Lecturer in Geography (2009), 'Environment: Project and Assignment Booklet, 2010', and from The Open University's StudentHome Study Skills website (internal access only).)

In our example, you would need to discuss whether the family in Britain is in crisis. There is an implicit *claim* here: 'the family is in crisis'; and an implicit counter-claim: 'the family is not in crisis'. Your job, then, is to consider the evidence. This might include data on the percentage of children in foster care compared with 10 or 20 or 50 years ago – which might lead you to consider changes to policy on social services interventions – or you might focus on the changing roles of men and women in the domestic and social spheres – and the evidence (or not) that this has had an impact on children's upbringing – or, you may argue that the traditional notion of the family is something of a 'myth' . . . As you can see, there are a variety of ways to tackle the question, and being asked to 'discuss' the claim gives you scope to consider a range of evidence, using the concepts and theories introduced on your module.

4.3   Types of social science essay questions

Broadly speaking, there are three 'types' of questions in the social sciences: advocacy, compare and contrast, and evaluation questions. These types of question suggest particular formats, or structures, for your essay answers. At the earlier and later stages of your studies, the different types of questions will require different skills and, therefore, different sorts of answers.

Advocacy questions

Advocacy questions ask you to outline or explain and illustrate a single issue, topic or argument. You might think of them as 'making a case' for a particular idea. Examples of this kind of question would include:

- How have changes to the way in which the production of food is organized affected both the UK and other parts of the world? Illustrate your answer with relevant examples.

- 'An efficient allocation of resources requires fiscal neutrality, yet the British tax system persists in encouraging some activities while discouraging others.' Explain and illustrate with examples.
- What is the role of the judiciary in the law-making process? Include a discussion of statutory interpretation and the system of precedent.
- What are the basic assumptions about humanistic psychology? How are these reflected in methods for encouraging growth?

Advocacy answers

A basic answer to an advocacy question might look something like this:

Introduction

- Indicate the broad content of your essay.
- Indicate what you see as the core issue(s) and how you intend to approach this (these) – in other words, say what you will be 'advocating' or speaking about.

Main section

- Provide a brief overview of the issue, topic or argument. Depending on the length of the essay, you may have space to include some contextualization of the issue as well.
- Provide a more detailed breakdown of the key components of the issue, topic or argument – in other words, develop your 'case'.
- Give examples to illustrate these points.
- Briefly explore weaknesses in the viewpoint that you've been asked to advocate and indicate alternative ways of thinking about the issues.

Or, as another example, you may decide to do the following:

- Provide a brief overview of the issue, topic or argument.
- Then, in more detail, make your 'case': outline one component of the issue, topic or argument and illustrate with an example; outline the second component of the issue, topic or argument and illustrate with another relevant example; outline the third component, etc.
- Briefly explore weaknesses in the approach and indicate alternative ways of addressing the issues.

The nature of the question and the material you have chosen to use will dictate the structure of an advocacy answer. However, it will generally be expected that you will build a 'case' in a logical and convincing manner.

Conclusion

- Recap key points and illustrations. Give a final assessment of the usefulness of the approach.

Remember, this is only a basic format covering the major ingredients of an advocacy question and you shouldn't follow it slavishly.

Advocacy questions in relation to 'introductory', 'intermediate' and 'advanced' essay writing

Advocating a position is one of the more basic undergraduate essay writing skills. As you develop 'intermediate' and 'advanced' skills, you will be expected to show an increasing ability to outline and illustrate more complex positions, a greater understanding of their potential weaknesses, and an increased awareness of alternative ways of addressing the issues.

Compare and contrast questions

Compare and contrast questions ask you to: outline points of common ground between competing positions; explore ways in which they differ, identifying how different positions often appeal to different kinds of evidence; and, sometimes, compare the particular positions to other positions in the same field. Examples of this kind of question would include:

- Compare and contrast two different explanations of 'racial' divisions.
- Contrast the argument that today's globalization is mainly about the production of flows, with the argument that prioritizes territories.
- Compare and contrast Lacanian and 'British School' psychoanalytic accounts of identity formation.

Compare and contrast answers

A basic answer to a compare and contrast question might look something like this:

Introduction

- Indicate the broad content of the essay.
- Outline the comparisons you intend to make – the key areas of common ground and the differences between the issues/positions, etc.

Main text

- Outline position (a) and position (b).
- Identify key points of common ground between these positions and compare them.

- Identify supplementary points of common ground between these positions and compare them.
- Identify and explore key points of contrast between position (a) and position (b).
- Identify and explore supplementary points of contrast between position (a) and position (b).
- If necessary, identify and explore significant ways in which position (a) and position (b) can be contrasted to a third competing position (c).
- Briefly evaluate the merits of these positions.

Once again, you will almost certainly need to adapt this basic format to fit different questions and different material. For instance:

- There may be an obvious debate 'behind' the question that requires you to emphasize the ways in which two contrasting positions share a common orientation that is in competition with a third position.
- This might be the case in the third of the example questions. It reads: 'Compare and contrast Lacanian and "British School" psychoanalytic accounts of identity formation.' Here you might need to emphasize that competing psychoanalytic approaches share a common belief in the importance of unconscious processes, a belief not shared by, for example, ethnomethodological, Foucauldian and some other social constructionist accounts. A debate of this kind may require you to scale down the extent to which you compare and contrast positions (a) and (b) in order for you to contrast them to a third position (c).
- Equally, you may decide to compare a key point from positions (a) and (b) and then move straight on to contrast a key point from each position. You would then compare another point and contrast another point, and so on. This would be an alternative to exploring all the points of comparison in one section and then all the points of contrast in another. Ask yourself which method works best in relation to the question set and the material with which you are working.

The trick is to adapt this basic structure to a shape that best fits your requirements.

Conclusion

- Summarize the major points of comparison and contrast between the positions and briefly recap which is the most persuasive and why.

Compare and contrast questions in relation to 'introductory', 'intermediate' and 'advanced' essay writing

There is likely to be an increased expectation that you will be able to compare and contrast positions and arguments as you move beyond your introductory studies. In developing 'intermediate' and 'advanced' skills you will be expected to show: an increasing ability to compare and contrast more complex positions; a greater sophistication in your analysis and a greater ability to emphasize key points; a greater confidence in showing a reasoned preference for one position over another; the ability to write from 'within' one or another position; and an increasing ability to relate the positions under analysis to relevant alternative positions in the same field.

Evaluation questions

As noted above, evaluation questions ask you to examine arguments for and against a particular position or issue and to assess their relative strengths and weaknesses. Examples of this kind of question would include:

- To what extent does citizenship depend on having a modern welfare state?
- 'Conceptual categories are clearly defined and tightly structured as hierarchically organized mental representations.' How far do you agree with this view?
- Critically evaluate the definition of work as paid employment.
- Select a healthcare policy that relates to your own area of nursing practice. Discuss the origins of the policy, its authorship and how it has been developed. Critically examine the context of the policy and to what and to whom the policy relates, and identify its potential to impact positively on patient and client care.

Evaluation answers

A basic answer to an evaluation question might look something like this:

Introduction

- Indicate the broad content of the essay.
- Briefly express the considerations that will go into your evaluation.

Main section

- Outline the position(s) or issue(s).
- Give arguments (that is, chains of logical reasoning) and evidence in support of the position.
- Give arguments supported by evidence that go against, question or show limitations to the position.
- Weigh up the arguments for and against the position.

In the light of different material and different questions you may well want to adapt this basic format. For instance:

- You might start with the 'weaker' of the arguments in the main section and follow it up with 'stronger' arguments. Will this convince the reader of your point of view more effectively?
- Rather than exploring the first position (a) then the second and competing position (b), you could explore one point from position (a) and contrast it with a parallel point from position (b), then explore another point from position (a) and contrast it with another point from position (b), and so on. Does this clarify or confuse your overall argument?

As with answers to advocacy or compare and contrast questions, you will need to decide how best to structure the argument in light of the question asked and the material used to answer it. Equally, you will need to emphasize different sections (the exploration of arguments for and against, the evaluation section) depending on the nature of the question.

As before, the trick is to adapt this basic structure to a shape that best fits your requirements.

Conclusion

- Summarize, making an explicit statement as to which position (if any) you find most convincing (given the evidence and logic of the argument) and to what extent, or with what caveats.

Evaluation questions in relation to 'introductory', 'intermediate' and 'advanced' essay writing

As a skill, evaluation is undoubtedly more challenging than advocacy. In consequence, in developing 'intermediate' and 'advanced' skills, you will be expected to show an increasing ability to evaluate more complex or nuanced positions, increased awareness of alternative ways of addressing the issues, and more confidence in showing a reasoned preference for one position over another. Additionally, although not in all circumstances, you will be expected to demonstrate the ability to write from 'within' a perspective or theory. This means, on the basis of an informed academic judgement, adopting the conceptual world-view of a perspective or theory and evaluating competing perspectives and theories through the 'lens' of this world-view (see Section 8.2).

37

Summary

- Make sure you have read the question, which involves 'unpacking' its different parts.
- Social sciences questions are frequently in two parts: 'process' or 'command' words and 'content' words.
- Command words reflect the different cognitive skills being tested in a given essay.
- Advocacy questions ask you to outline and illustrate a particular issue, topic or argument.
- Compare and contrast questions ask you to identify and explore points of comparison and contrast between competing positions.
- Evaluation questions ask you to explore arguments for and against competing positions and to evaluate their relative strengths and weaknesses.
- Suggested structures should be adapted in the light of the question and the material under discussion.
- As you develop 'intermediate' and 'advanced' skills you will be expected to show greater confidence and ability in deploying essay structuring skills. Your essays will also need to demonstrate more nuanced, complex and comprehensive understanding.

Self-test

1 What is the most common reason for a well-written essay to receive a low mark?
2 What is a 'content' word?
3 What is a 'process' or 'command' word?
4 As you move into intermediate- and advanced-level studies, what sorts of cognitive skills will your essays increasingly test?
5 What is: an 'advocacy'; a 'compare and contrast'; an 'evaluation' question?
6 What are the similarities and differences between the suggested basic structures of advocacy, compare and contrast, and evaluation questions?

5

Reading, Note-taking and Literature Searches

- Reading
- Taking notes
- Academic literature searches and gathering data
- The perils of using the internet
- The pleasures of using the internet

Before you begin writing your essay, or even planning to write your essay, you will have done quite a lot of preparation. This chapter outlines what that preparation will entail, but it cannot describe in detail all of the activities students undertake as part of their studies – for that, you may wish to look at other books that cover, for instance, university-level study skills, or literature searches. Instead, we look at the work that is core to preparing for essay writing.

5.1 Reading

Without a doubt the most crucial skill that you will need to deploy in preparing to write an essay is reading, closely followed by note-taking. Strong writers are generally effective and often avid readers. Reading academic material has a number of purposes – such as preparing for a seminar, gaining general familiarity with a new subject, or filling in 'gaps' in your knowledge related to a specific lecture or seminar. However, here we are going to focus on a very instrumental approach to reading: purposeful reading to prepare for essay writing.

There are two main sorts of purposeful reading for essay writing – the first is 'skim' reading, the second is deeper or 'close' reading. Skim reading involves looking at a book, article, chapter or website at a glance. The idea is to get a quick sense of whether the source is going to be useful for your purposes.

With a recommended textbook, you can begin by looking up a key word in the contents pages and finding the relevant chapter. Remember you are trying to find out information that will help you with your essay, so:

- keep your essay title on a piece of paper in front of you while you are reading.

Here is an example of an essay question from a social sciences course on Environment:

According to the 1992 GATT (General Agreement on Tariffs and Trade) report, trade and environment are 'mutually supportive'. To what extent does the global trade in Colombian roses support this claim?

The required textbook for the module includes a chapter entitled, 'Trading with the environment', by Annie Taylor.

- Read the introductory paragraph.

One wet morning in December 1999, a crowd of about 50,000 people gathered on the streets of downtown Seattle. It was to become a historic protest, the first of many similar large-scale demonstrations. There were representatives from a huge range of groups: US steelworkers, consumer groups, development groups such as Oxfam, environmentalists such as the Royal Society for the Protection of Birds and Friends of the Earth, and animal rights groups. And it was not just organized groups – there were also individuals with no organized base. The real importance of the protest lies in the fact that so many people came together with a shared and unshakeable belief that the cause of the problems on which they were campaigning related to economic globalization and more particularly to the management of global trade. They chose Seattle on the first three days of December 1999 . . . because that is where the World Trade Organization (WTO) was holding its Annual Ministerial Meeting.

(*Source:* Taylor, A. (2003) 'Trading with the environment', in Bingham, N., Blowers, A. and Belshaw, C. (eds), *Contested Environments*, Milton Keynes/Chichester, OU/Wiley, p. 172.)

On the surface of it, there is little here that relates directly to the essay question. There is something about global trade that sounds promising and a mention of environmentalists. In short, on the basis of the introduction to this chapter, we can't be sure it will be helpful.

- The next stage is to look up key words in the index or, if the source is online, using a key word search.

There are a number of content words in this essay question: GATT, (global) trade, environment and Colombian roses. If we look in the book's index for 'GATT' there are five citations, including two specifically on the Report on Trade and the Environment. 'Global trade' has lots of citations, but three that are on roses. 'Environment' also has lots of citations, including two on environment and global trade. 'Roses' has three citations linked with global trade, as well as a number of other citations. This chapter looks now to be quite useful, despite the unpromising introduction.

- You might now decide to 'skim read' the chapter, noting particularly helpful sections.

There are different techniques for skim reading: reading the first and last paragraphs in a chapter, then the first and last lines in each 'promising' section, as identified by your index search; scanning through the whole piece, looking out for key authors, words or phrases and reading the paragraphs nearest these; reading only the paragraphs or pages of the chapter that you have found in your index search.

Skim reading is particularly useful if you are still not certain that the text will help you with your essay. Skim reading can also be an efficient way of finding pithy quotes, or examples to support your argument. Where you find particularly helpful sections, remember to note precisely where they are (i.e. page numbers), and how you think they might help you when you come to write your essay.

Using the tactic above, I have found a short paragraph on the effects of rose production on the environment that could support the counter-argument that global trade is *not* supportive of the environment:

Forests are cleared to make room for the farms. Once the farms are operating the flowers need lots of water to make them grow and the rose farms draw heavily from local water supplies. Around the town of Madrid in Colombia the water level in the aquifer has fallen from 20 metres to 200 metres, and water now has to come from Bogotá. The pesticides and fertilizers, if not properly treated, run off to pollute local rivers. Because local farmers use the river water for their agriculture, the local produce that they live off – vegetables, grains and grazing pasture livestock – are also affected. (Taylor, 2003, p. 174)

Again scanning, I saw a neat phrase that could be used in a sentence that supports a balanced approach to trade and environment. Taylor says that 'trade is not an unquestionable villain' (Taylor, 2003, p. 176). I like the sound of this phrase and, if I decide that the evidence supports the balanced view, I think I would be hard pressed to find a pithier way to express this.

- Read critically and with purpose.

Once you have decided that the chapter (or article, or webpage) is going to be useful, you will want to read most or all of it, with purpose and with an analytical or critical approach (see Section 6.1). In part, this means being an active reader: 'interrogating' the text, and being 'physical' with it, asking critical questions as you read and taking notes (see Section 5.2) that will be useful for your essay. Active reading is a skill that you can develop, and is essential to good social science practice.

Tom Burns and Sandra Sinfield, who are specialist lecturers in learning development at London Metropolitan University, suggest some generic questions you should ask yourself as you begin reading in more depth. These are set in a grid below to help you organize your thoughts:

Essay question: *According to the 1992 GATT (General Agreement on Tariffs and Trade) report, trade and environment are 'mutually supportive'. To what extent does the global trade in Colombian roses support this claim?*

Essay topic (1): *For this bit of reading, I am going to focus on the claim that:* 'the production of roses for global trade is mutually supportive of the environment'.	Author/title of article/contents (Reference) Taylor, A. (2003) 'Trading with the environment', in Bingham, N., Blowers, A. and Belshaw, C. (eds), *Contested Environments*. OU/Wiley, Milton Keynes/Chichester.
Why am I reading this?	I need to know more about why rose production for global trade might be environmentally harmful/helpful/neutral.

What am I looking for?	Evidence that the production of roses is: 1 supportive of the environment 2 environmentally neutral (or there are benefits of trade that outweigh the harm) 3 not supportive of the environment Arguments: 1 Pros and cons of the global trade in roses (more theoretical) 2 Names of authors and theorists who have written on this subject Supplementary material: 1 Pithy quotes that can enliven my writing
How will I use the information?	As I read through the chapter, I can make notes in the margin of the book (if I own it), or in my notebook, following the broad outline of 'what am I looking for?' I can mark up the text with 'evidence: rose production/trade harmful to environment', or 'argument: free trade helps development', etc.
Where will I use the information?	The short answer is 'in my essay', but see below for a more detailed approach to this.
Which bit of my assignment will it help me with?	This will depend on how I structure my essay. To get started, I think I will organize the essay into three main parts: 1 Arguments that global trade is damaging to the environment, with specific evidence from the trade in and production of roses. 2 Arguments that global trade can bring benefits to the environment or other benefits that outweigh the harm to the environment, with specific evidence from the trade in and production of roses. 3 A discussion that weighs up the evidence for and against in light of an analysis of the different vested interests in a) continuing global trade and b) environmental conservation.

(Continued)

(Continued)

	Alternatively, I might organize the information by key word – so, I will use my reading to expand my knowledge on global trade, Colombian rose production, etc.
How will I know when I have what I need?	This is the tricky bit, particularly for social scientists, who tend to find more questions the more they read. However, there are two pragmatic answers: 1 When I can meet the requirements of this section of the assignment, according to whether I have addressed the different elements of the circuit of knowledge. So, I need to ask: whether I have gathered strong (well-supported) evidence, and counter-evidence; can I explain the arguments or claims of the different proponents; can I explain the concepts used to develop this topic? 2 When I have run out of time. This highly pragmatic approach may surprise you, but it is a reality of essay writing that you will have a deadline to meet.

(*Source:* Adapted from: Burns, T. and Sinfield, S. (2008) *Essential Study Skills*, London/ Thousand Oaks, Sage, p. 159.)

Once you have your reading objectives in mind, you can start to read analytically and critically. This kind of active reading ensures that you remain engaged with the text and will help you remember what you have read. As you read, ask yourself the following questions. If you are doing a close reading, you can ask these questions of each paragraph.

- What is the main idea here? The main topic of a paragraph is usually revealed in the first sentence (sometimes called the 'topic sentence'). Highlight the main (topic,) word (or phrase,) or write . . . (it out) in the margin. . . .
- What is the author's argument? . . .

- Where is the author coming from? Are they on the left or the right? Are they Marxist or (neo-conservative) . . .? Are they (free-market liberals or radical environmentalists) . . .? Do they have a feminist perspective? . . .
- Have I encountered this argument before? Where? Make a note of who else would support this view. . . .
- Have I encountered a different argument somewhere? Where? Again, make connections, and notice consciously counter arguments. . . .
- What evidence is being offered? Highlight it or make a note. . . .
- Is the evidence valid? Why do I think it is or is not valid? Make notes. . . .
- How does this change what I have already read/heard? Cross-referencing in this way is very active reading. Ask yourself, now what do I think? . . .
- What is the author's final point? Usually the 'point' is in the final sentence of a paragraph. Notice what the author intended the paragraph to do. . . .

(*Source:* Adapted from: Burns, T. and Sinfield, S. (2008) *Essential Study Skills*, London/ Thousand Oaks, Sage, pp. 160–1.)

Read the following excerpt from Kate Nash's (2009) article, on citizenship and human rights:

Super-citizens

Within the legal status of 'full citizenship' there is a marked difference between what we might call 'super-citizens' and 'marginal citizens' in relation to human rights. Super-citizens have all the rights of citizens but increasingly, in a globalizing, deregulated political economy, citizenship does not tie them to states because they own the means of production or are in possession of secure employment or marketable skills that enable mobility across borders. Super-citizens are those Craig Calhoun calls 'frequent flier' elite cosmopolitans (Calhoun, 2003).

This group has very little material interest as a group in human rights except insofar as human rights policies may succeed in making the world generally more stable and profitable. Their protected mobility comes from their citizenship status as well as from their wealth and/or skills. When faced with unstable or dangerous political conditions, super-citizens are more likely to fly home or to appeal to the authorities of the states to which they belong to intervene on their behalf than they are to claim human rights. On the other hand, they may be more likely to identify with cosmopolitanism and human rights than other people. Super-citizens may be involved in the extension of human rights as professionals – especially as lawyers, leaders of International Non-Governmental Organizations, or researchers – though they would not generally expect to see themselves as the subjects of human rights claims. With a cool detachment from de-moded nationalist fervour, they may also be more likely than others to celebrate specifically cosmopolitan virtues, including the adherence to principles of individual human rights (Turner, 2002).

(*Source*: Nash, Kate, (2009) 'Between citizenship and human rights', *Sociology*, vol. 43, no. 6, Dec., pp. 1067–83, p. 1073.)

Here is our summary of the excerpt, using Burns' and Sinfield's prompts:

- The first sentence suggests that 'human rights' are unevenly available, depending on whether one is a 'super-citizen' or 'marginal citizen'.
- Super-citizens have global mobility due to employment skills or other status, and, due to financial security, may not see themselves as needing 'human rights' protection.
- From this section, the author's 'take' or 'position' is not clear, but Nash may be arguing against a simplistic understanding of 'cosmopolitanism'. There is an area of globalization research that looks at cosmopolitanism as a noticeable feature of contemporary political and cultural engagement.
- She cites Turner and Calhoun, but does she agree with Calhoun?
- There is no direct evidence for her claims, but Nash cites Turner regarding the ways super-citizens might see themselves in relation to cosmopolitanism and human rights. N.B. May need to *look up Turner*.
- The final sentence argues that super-citizens embrace cosmopolitanism and believe in individual human rights.

You may have noticed other key ideas, or summarized this section somewhat differently; perhaps your field is in human rights or globalization and you bring with you background understandings that inflect your reading. The point here is to think about *how* you read, and to help yourself read actively. Having read the rest of the article, or found out more about what Calhoun or Turner have to say, the thoughts above may well be revised – reading actively, however, enables this.

5.2   Taking notes

You will have gathered from the previous section that taking notes is integral to active – and therefore productive – reading. Note-taking is quite a personal thing, but there is good evidence to suggest that the more active you are in taking notes in your own words, the more you will recall. Generally speaking, you should write questions, comments and translations of material into your own words as much as possible. How you form your notes, however, will depend on a number of factors. As our purpose in this book is to prepare you for essay-writing, we will focus on those note-taking techniques most productive for short-term memory and making useful materials accessible for writing.

- Notes for essays should be selective. In other words, you should try to focus on the material that is most relevant for your assignment, ignoring more peripheral material, however interesting it may be.
- They should also be short. There is no point in simply rewriting the whole of a chapter. You are better off writing a summary, with a clear citation so you can go back to the original text if you need to.
- With the exception of direct quotations (which should be short and used sparingly), notes should be in your own words as this helps retention and is an important stage in essay writing.
- Notes for essays should be well-organized and clearly written so that you can refer back to them easily.

Note-taking on your own books

Hopefully, you will already be familiar with marking up your textbooks with a variety of notes in the margins – comments, questions, connections with other authors, etc. (Please remember, though, if you don't own the text, you should photocopy the pages before scribbling to your heart's content.) When it comes to writing your essays, however, margin notes are not very accessible.

Note-taking in notebooks or on index cards

Because margin notes are great at helping retention, but less good for helping you organize an example or argument in preparation for essay writing, you will need to develop additional note-taking strategies. Some students prefer to make notes in notebooks, adopting a 'linear' or 'outline' style – lists with headings and sub-headings. This is a helpful technique to summarize chapters, articles, lectures, etc. and is easy to refer to when you come to do your writing.

@ A recent lecture on the website TED (www.ted.com), 'On the art of choosing', by Sheena Iyengar, might be summarized in linear form like this:

1 Iyengar suggests that choice and the usefulness of different choices are culturally inflected.

2 Examples/evidence:

  a green tea with sugar
  b children doing an anagram task
  c selection of drinks/sodas
  d life support for severely ill infants

3 Iyengar sets out to challenge a number of key assumptions:

  a We do best when we choose for ourselves
  b More options = better choices
  c You must never say 'no' to choice

4 Americans in particular carry a positive narrative of 'limitless choice':

  a But not everyone/everywhere sees limitless choice as positive
  b Americans might reconsider the value of this narrative, in light of the examples/evidence.

5 She closes with a paraphrase: 'A rose by any other name looks different and probably smells different.'

(*Source*: Iyengar, Sheena (2010) 'On the Art of Choosing', TED talks, filmed and posted July 2010, www.ted.com/talks/sheena_iyengar_on_the_art_of_choosing.html, Accessed 2 August 2010.)

Other students prefer to take 'mindmap' notes. (See, for example, Figure 6).

Index cards can also be used for either style of handwritten note-taking. Index cards are preferred by many students as they encourage 'thinking in shorthand'. Like any other paper-based notes, index cards can include lists, mindmaps, definitions, case studies, summaries of key theorists' ideas, etc. Index cards may have an advantage over notebook notes as they can be shuffled into different orders which may help you structure your thinking when preparing to write your essay.

Note-taking using computer software

There are a number of proprietary programmes, such as KnowledgeNotebook (www.knowledgenotebook.com/index.html), or Open Educational Resources (OERs) like FreeMind (http://sourceforge.net/projects/freemind/) that are

Here is the same lecture, but in mind map form:

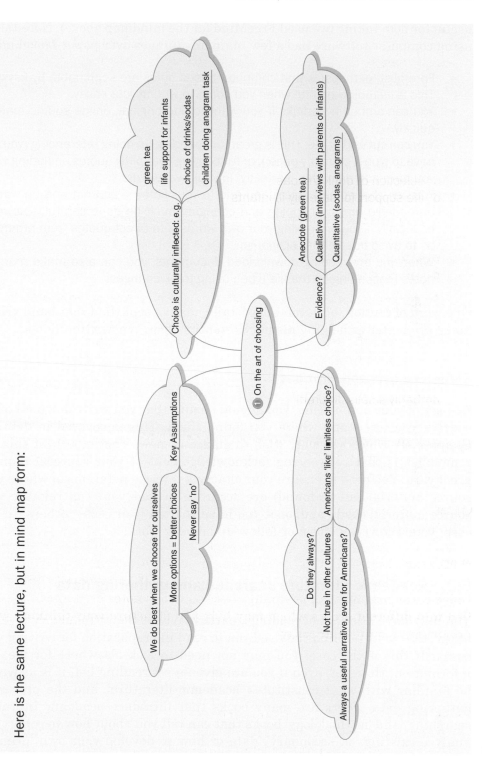

Figure 6 Mindmap for 'On the Art of Choosing' by Sheena Iyengar (2010).

useful for note-taking (we used FreeMind for the mindmap above). Note-taking using computer software has a few main advantages over paper-based notes:

- Foremost, perhaps, is that computer-based notes are searchable by keyword. This is incredibly helpful when you come to writing your essay.
- You can embed hyperlinks if you want to find original, online source material quickly.
- You can cut and paste. This is great for speeding up doing referencing (you only have to type it correctly once!), or for copying over pithy quotes, including when you have noted an idea 'perfectly' in your own words.
- You can change and delete and add to your notes – and not end up with an unreadable mess. Chopping and changing must be done carefully, however, especially if you are mixing your own words with direct quotes from others, so as to avoid inadvertent plagiarism.
- When you are reading downloaded documents, you can also make marginal notes (depending on the file type), using track changes.

One word of caution, however: anecdotally, many people find that handwritten notes are better at helping memory retention than typewritten notes.

Reference lists and citations

As part of your note-taking, you should ensure that you write down all of the sources you use – and where you found them. This is covered in detail in Chapter 10, which you may wish to glance at now. The important thing to remember is that referencing (acknowledgement of your sources) requires great care. You need to ensure your citations (precise notations of where your source material can be found) are accurate so that your can relocate your source material easily and, once you have written your essay, others (in this case, your tutor) can check or follow up on your work.

5.3 Academic literature searches and gathering data

You may have a set list of readings, particularly at the introductory levels of study, that your tutor has advised you to read in preparation for writing your essay. If this is the case, you may not need to look elsewhere for ideas or information. However, even if you are given a set reading list, it is as well to be familiar with what constitutes 'academic literature', and the process of gathering data. There are many books that introduce academic literature searching, and 'methodology' books that can tell you about how to collect and analyse existing, or 'secondary', data or how to develop your own 'primary' data. It is not the purpose of this book to replace the more detailed advice you can find in such texts; however, having an awareness of the process, and developing your skills as a social scientist will help you enormously when you come to write essays. For this reason, we provide a short summary of what's involved.

Academic literature Searches

In short, a literature search means browsing the writing that *already exists* in your field of study. But it is also more than this, because at the end of a literature search you should have a(n):

* knowledge of the broad field of research in the area;
* understanding of the main theories, concepts and debates that have shaped the field;
* knowledge of more specific research and theorizing on your chosen topic;
* set of notes on what you have found;
* list of key theorists and their ideas, as well as counter-ideas;
* set of appropriately tagged bookmarks (on Del-icio-us, for instance);
* full and accurate set of references (organized in EndNote or RefWorks, for instance).

The extent of your literature search will depend on a number of factors, most especially how much time you have.

We will consider the joys and perils of using online resources such as Wikipedia (http://wikipedia.org) in a moment. Let's assume, though, that you have looked up your topics in Wikipedia, so you have a baseline of non-peer-reviewed (we'll come back to this) information about your set topic. Now we'll look at more traditional social science resources. These come in a number of different forms: single author 'monographs', edited collections, journal articles, conference papers, official government or NGO (non-governmental organization) publications or statistical websites and reference books.

Some books are 'textbooks' – in other words they are specifically designed to be useful for teaching and are written for a novice readership. In these, you will find overviews of main topics, or theories. The most basic of these are titles like *Chomsky for Beginners* (Cogswell, 2007) or *Understanding Representation* (Webb, 2009). If you are in your first year or so of university, these sorts of texts can be immensely useful. But you will be able to tell by the slimness of the volume, the slow pace of explanations or the lack of original writing (i.e. not the original author of the ideas presented) that these will not be *as* helpful to you later on in your studies, nor are they adequate for more in-depth research on a particular subject. So, how do you find the 'right' kind of book, conference paper or journal article? The simple answer is: go to your university library.

When searching the university's library catalogue, you will need to be adept at focusing your research on particular topics. Identifying the content words in your essay question is a good place to start (see Chapter 4).

Overview: Sources of information

Before you read, you need to choose what to read very carefully. Tick the activities you have undertaken.

- Books:

  - ☐ I have found some of the books on the reading list and looked at them. . .

- Contents pages:

  - ☐ I have looked for a word from the assignment question in the Contents pages.
  - ☐ I have chosen which sections of the book(s) to read.
  - ☐ I have gauged how much time I will need to read and take notes on these sections.

- Indexes:

  - ☐ I have looked for the word in the Index at the back of the book.
  - ☐ I have looked at these pages and decided I will/will not read more of that book.

- Wider searches:

  - ☐ I have used the electronic catalogue in my library – the key word, author or subject search facilities.
  - ☐ I have found a couple of books and repeated the above with them.
  - ☐ I have used the following search engines or bookmarking networks.

- Help – I have asked the following people for assistance:

  - ☐ my tutor
  - ☐ other students
  - ☐ the subject librarian
    - ☐ who has directed me to:
    - ☐ these search engines . . .
    - ☐ these journals/online journals . . .

☐ these websites for my subject.
☐ my online study network.

(*Source*: Adapted from: Burns, T. and Sinfield, S. (2008) *Essential Study Skills*, London/ Thousand Oaks, Sage, pp. 157–8.)

As you expand your searches beyond the recommended reading on your set lists, an important part of your task is to ensure that the material you look at is credible. There are techniques for determining this. Your tutor will have done some of the work for you and you can assume that the readings on your recommended or further reading lists are credible; likewise, you can assume that the authors your tutor refers to most often, or those most cited within your set texts, are worth reading. But beyond this, you need to rely on the shared conventions of the social sciences academy.

Peer review

You may have heard the term 'peer reviewed'. This simply means that an article or conference paper has been subject to scrutiny by other academics in the same subject area as the author of the article or paper. Although there are debates about the impact of the peer-review system on innovation and debate in academia, it is generally seen as the best way to ensure that research is rigorous and that academic claims are well-argued and well-supported (see for instance, www.timeshighereducation.co.uk/story.asp?sectioncode=26&storycode=412600). Your tutor will likely guide you mostly to peer-reviewed articles – and when you do your own searches, you should prioritize peer-reviewed sources.

Gathering data

Academic literature searches involve looking at what other people have written and researched. When you come to write about their research, it becomes 'secondary' material – in other words, you are reporting on it 'second hand' as you did not do the research yourself. Primary data, on the other hand, is data that you have yourself created. This might take the form of an interview, a content analysis or a close reading of a film clip, etc. Where an essay question asks for examples or illustrative material you should clarify with your tutor whether these should be examples researched or cited by others, or whether you should conduct your own research. Part of the purpose of doing a literature search is to see if anyone else has already done the research you are embarking on. If they have, it could be that your primary research will add to the weight of their argument; conversely, it could be that your research will throw into question some of the existing findings. Or it could be that social circumstances have changed and that what was claimed before no longer holds true. Knowing what empirical data has already been published, and what claims about it have already been made will shape the kind of research – or primary data creation – you choose to do.

The perils of using the internet

'Wikipedia is a curse to higher education.' Discuss

As far as we know, this hasn't been set as an essay title, but perhaps it should be. Many tutors despair at finding references to Wikipedia in their students' essays, in part because Wikipedia is not a peer-reviewed source and the material posted to Wikipedia can be unreliable or inaccurate. Worse is when students don't reference Wikipedia, and yet it is obvious that it is a main source of material for an essay. Worse still, however, is the use of non-referenced articles or even whole essays which are available on the internet. In Chapter 11, we discuss the problems with plagiarism and how to avoid it, but for now, we will focus on what is particularly problematic about using material from non-academic internet websites, such as Wikipedia.

- Material is not peer-reviewed in the traditional academic sense and risks therefore being inaccurate or academically unsound in other ways.
- Much Wikipedia material is itself unreferenced, so students can end up drawing on a range of resources of which they are wholly unaware. A recent plagiarism case where the student had copied a page from Wikipedia revealed nine separate original resources, none of which were referenced on the Wikipedia site, nor, of course, in the student's essay.
- It is 'too easy' to cut and paste content, and simply forget to re-write in your own words, or to reference. This practice may be an acceptable way to bring together information in some primary and secondary schools, but is not acceptable in higher education.
- The internet is vast and without careful planning it is tremendously easy to waste a great deal of time on erroneous searches, or being distracted by interesting but irrelevant material.

The pleasures of using the internet

On the other hand, the internet *is* vast and provides access to a wealth of excellent social science resources. It is essential to become adept at using the internet for academic purposes, including making good use of search engines, such as Google Scholar (http://scholar.google.com), shared book-marking sites, like Del-icio-us (http://delicious.com/) or tools like RSS feeds (which route updates from selected sites directly to your email). Becoming a social scientist also means making good use of research and academic networks in your subject area and amongst your student colleagues. This may mean subscribing to your tutor's blog, or to recommended blogs by experts in your field, or to relevant social and academic networking sites.

Your university is likely to make use of a VLE (virtual learning environment), such as Moodle (http://moodle.org) for teaching and learning, and this will have resources such as referencing tools which can help you organize your references into the format required by your tutor, as well as having notes pages which are searchable by keyword.

If you have mainly used the internet for informal learning or social networking, you may find it helpful to learn a bit more about using it for research. One recommended site is 'Internet Detective' (www.vts.intute.ac.uk/detective) which is a free online tutorial that can help you develop academic research skills using the internet.

Summary

- Purposeful and active reading, which involves being able to scan material quickly, as well as reading in-depth and critically, is essential to good essay writing.
- Note-taking is part of active reading and helps you remember what you have read. It is also essential for helping you to see what material you have and what further material you will need to write your essay. Note-taking is a 'personal thing': linear or diagrammatic notes are both fine.
- You should make use of sources recommended by your tutor and focus on 'peer-reviewed' journals when conducting independent research.
- Primary data is data created and relayed by the original researcher.
- Secondary data is data that is reported second hand.
- Internet sources may not be credible and special caution should be used when cutting and pasting from online materials.
- Internet sources may be excellent and can expand your network of colleagues and subject knowledge.

Self-test

1 What sorts of questions can help you read 'analytically and critically'?
2 What are the advantages of taking notes on a computer? By hand?
3 Why do you think you should prioritize 'peer-reviewed' academic journal articles?
4 What are some of the risks associated with using material downloaded from the internet?

6

Thinking Critically and Formulating an Argument

- Critical thinking
- Formulating an argument

Much of this book focuses on relatively straightforward work you can do to improve your writing. Accurate citations, helpful notes, essay planning and a clear structure to your essay can make a big difference to your marks. However, to gain the top grades in any social science subject, you will need to develop your critical thinking skills and ability to formulate an argument. It is something that will take time and effort – but, if you are after top marks, it will be worth it.

6.1 Critical thinking

Chapter 2 (Section 2.2) introduced you to the circuit of knowledge, which is a useful tool for thinking critically, as a social scientist. Although some social science ideas and theories can be complex, the basic point of thinking like a social scientist is to consider the usefulness (strengths and weaknesses) of evidence and the power (logic, explanatory reach) of concepts, arguments and theories in making sense of our social world.

As we've discussed, you should approach your reading critically, for instance, to consider whether an author is making a convincing argument, whether there is a logic, or 'sense', to it and whether the evidence being cited adequately supports the claims made. When taking notes, you might try to compare one argument with another – or think about whether there are other issues or explanations that could be considered. When writing, an important part of your work will involve organizing your thoughts into a logical order, making coherent arguments that are backed up with sound evidence, and being attuned to any bias or preconceptions you might bring to your studies. In short, at every stage of your work, you should be engaged in critical thinking. But how to do this?

In Section 5.1, we looked at 'interrogating' your reading: asking a series of questions that will help you to understand the material more deeply. And the circuit of knowledge (Section 2.2) points up the importance of concepts and theories, and the use of evidence. Here we consider how to judge the evidence you select and the arguments you make, using a simple set of criteria:

- Validity;
- Reliability;
- Comprehensiveness; and
- Coherence.

In general, validity and reliability refer to the usefulness of evidence; comprehensiveness and coherence refer to the strength of concepts, arguments and theories.

Validity

'Validity' describes the degree to which data (evidence) measure or represent what they claim to measure or represent. Hugh MacKay and Paul Reynolds (2001, pp. 49–50) give this example:

> to test the hypothesis that mobile telephones, e-mail and other new communication technologies mean that we keep in closer touch with family and friends, we need to establish a direct relationship between use of the new technology and greater or closer contact with family and friends. It is not enough to claim a change in communication technology and to demonstrate an increased volume of use, and then to assume that this means that we keep in touch with family and friends more because, for instance, we might be contacting not family and friends but people we hardly know.

Reliability

Is the evidence you are citing specific to a particular time, date, group of people, or would the same results occur at a different time, on a different day, with a different group? To put it in the terms of the natural sciences: if an experiment were repeated, would it get the same results? If the answer is 'yes', then you can claim that the data are 'reliable'. Unfortunately, social science doesn't often afford the same control over variables that natural science does; in other words, it is difficult to replicate social science research exactly, time and again, because people and their social-environmental contexts change.

Comprehensiveness

'Comprehensiveness' describes the 'reach' of a claim. If we were to claim that 'there has been an increase in the use of door step grocery deliveries', we would need to clarify whether this is the case in both urban and rural areas, amongst men and women, wealthy and poor, and older and younger shoppers. If we find that all of these categories of shoppers have increased their use of door step grocery delivery, we can say that this is a comprehensive assertion, in other words, there is significant reach to the claim. Limited comprehensiveness is not a problem, however: the problem is claiming a greater comprehensiveness than there is evidence for.

Coherence

Is there a logic to the argument or claim, or are there inconsistencies or flaws in the argument, the concepts used or the assumptions behind the argument? Put in a slightly different way, we might think, as David Goldblatt does, about 'testing' accounts of society. He identifies three key features:

- the clarity of key claims and concepts,
- the logic of the chain of reasoning,
- and the plausibility and accuracy of the hidden assumptions behind the claims and reasoning.

(Adapted from: Goldblatt, D. (2000) cited in Mackay, H. et al. (2001), *Social Science in Action: Investigating the Information Society*, Milton Keynes/London, The Open University/Routledge, p. 51.)

6.2   Formulating an argument

How to formulate an argument brings us back to the circuit of knowledge and draws on your skills of critical thinking. Where you have been given an essay question, your argument will, to some extent, be determined for you. As

Section 2.2 and Chapter 4 point out, answering the question set is essential; but what if you have only been given a broad topic about which to write? In this case, you might be asking 'How do I work out what to say?' and the question of how to formulate an argument becomes all the more pressing.

At undergraduate level, there is less expectation that you will produce original research or thinking in your work. There is, however, an expectation that you will be able to utilize the original thinking of others in putting together a coherent essay. You should also, increasingly, be able to present the research findings of others correctly and to provide appropriate context so that your reader can understand the significance of any findings.

How do I work out what I want to say?

Without giving too pat an answer to this, one tried and tested way of developing your ideas about a social science topic is to focus on what Stuart Hall (and others) identifies as 'the differences that make a difference'. These include race, ethnicity, gender, sexuality, class, age, etc. Other 'matters that matter' might include urban or rural locations, cities or towns, employment, access to technologies, marital status, or the wealth or poverty of individuals or groups or their home nations.

You should be pragmatic about your choices. You will need to make use of the material presented on your module, and to consider the areas of interest of your tutor in determining the focus of your essay. In addition, you will need to gauge whether you have time to find sufficient material on your chosen topic and if those materials are easily accessible. This doesn't mean you should always choose 'safe' subjects, just that you should be realistic about what can be achieved in the given time.

Often, this means narrowing your focus.

Let's say you are taking a module on 'Women and Technology' and your tutor has set a 2,000-word essay around women and mobile technologies. Looking at the set readings, you find material on women and mobile phones, but nothing on women and laptops, or sat navs. Also, the readings mainly cite research conducted in the US and Australia, but nothing on developing nations. Narrowing your focus and finding a point of interest could involve comparing Australian women's uptake of mobile phones with satellite navigation, and comparing the different reasons for their use. Alternatively, you might be interested in whether the uptake and use of mobile phones is different for women in the US and Brazil. Another alternative might be to consider whether women's use of mobiles is different depending on age. Hopefully you can see that the 'differences that make a difference' have guided these suggestions.

Once you have your topic, you should now, effectively, set yourself an essay question. Throughout this book, we've introduced different sorts of essay question and in Sections 4.2 and 4.3 we looked at how different types of questions are intended to test different sorts of knowledge and skills. This is something you can consider when developing your own question. Will it be 'enough' to ask for a straightforward description? Will your tutor expect you to be able to evaluate evidence, or two (or more) competing theories at this stage in your studies? Has there been much emphasis on independent reading, or are you expected to make full use only of the set texts?

Taking one of the examples above – women's use of mobile phones depending on age – we could come up with a range of essay questions, some more appropriate at the earlier stages of study, some testing more advanced skills.

- Identify the key differences in the use of mobile phones for women in the 18–25 and 50–65 age range. (1,000 words)
- Explain some of the key reasons why the use of mobile phones may differ between women of 18–25 and those in the 50–65 age range. (1,500 words)
- 'Mobile phone use is core to younger women's identities, more so than for older women.' Evaluate this claim. (2,000 words)

There is a clear progression of skills, and word limits, in these examples. The first example requires simple description, and though you might be tempted to make comparisons this is not an explicit requirement. The second asks for more information: in order to explain, you would need first to state the differences and provide some reasons why those differences exist. You are implicitly required to compare. The third is certainly the most difficult as it requires some description of different uses of mobile phones, as well as some explanation, but more than this, there is a requirement to consider both the merits of any evidence and to explore theories of identity (and technology).

Summary

- Thinking critically is essential in social science work and will help you to achieve higher marks.
- Critical thinking is something you should do actively whilst reading and note-taking and should be demonstrated in your essay writing, particularly at intermediate and advanced levels.

(Continued)

(Continued)

- There are four simple 'criteria' you can use to judge the usefulness of evidence and the power of concepts, arguments and theories. These are: validity, reliability, comprehensiveness and coherence.
- Validity – the data presented measures what it claims to measure.
- Reliability – if repeated under the same conditions, the 'experiment' will yield the same results. This is difficult for social science as social conditions change and are not easily controlled.
- Comprehensiveness – the 'reach' of a theory or claim. It is fine to have limited comprehensiveness.
- Coherence – the logic of an argument or theory, and the assumptions behind an argument or theory.
- Formulating an argument requires careful ordering in a logical sequence.
- Deciding what to write about in the social sciences can often be guided by the 'differences that make a difference' or the 'matters that matter'.
- Developing your own essay question should involve consideration of your level of study and the sorts of skills and knowledge you think your tutor is interested in testing.

Self-test

1. What are validity and reliability concerned with?
2. What are comprehensiveness and coherence concerned with?
3. What are the 'differences that make a difference'?
4. How might you make a broad area of inquiry into a social science question?
5. How might you make an area of inquiry into a more challenging social science question?

7

Writing Introductions

- Longer or 'full' introductions
- Basic short introductions
- When do you write the introduction?

There are, of course, many ways to write an essay introduction. In this chapter, we will be exploring one of these, an approach that treats the introduction like an 'abstract' or brief synopsis of the central points raised in the essay, and that 'signposts' what you intend to say. The introduction-as-synopsis will cover just about everything that an effective introduction should achieve and will do this using a minimum number of words, an important consideration when the number of words available to you is limited. Having mastered this style of introduction, you will probably want to move on to writing introductions that are more creative.

You should not, therefore, feel obliged to follow these guidelines slavishly. Indeed, there is a danger that too rigid an interpretation of the advice in this chapter will cause your introductions to become dry and formulaic. As such, they may fail to grab your reader's attention. Academic writers often attempt to avoid this problem by, for example, beginning an article or chapter with an arresting quotation, image or challenging statement. Alternatively, they may start with a short discussion of an example or theme central to the matter in hand and use this to raise or signpost the questions to be addressed in the work that follows.

You may want to look for these and similar strategies in your reading. You may also wish to check the length of introductions. A general rule is that the introduction should account for between 5 and 10 per cent of the overall word count — but you will notice that in professional academic writing there is some considerable variation.

Like other areas of essay writing, you will probably find that you get better at introductions the more experienced you become. It is certainly fair to say that essays set at more advanced levels will expect more from your introductions than those at the introductory level. An introductory level essay should be able to identify the essay's subject and begin to highlight its key themes or arguments. More advanced essays should display a firm grasp of the central debates that lie 'behind' the question and provide a more sophisticated indication of the arguments it will develop. Sometimes more advanced essays will also need to 'establish a position' in the introduction, indicating that they are being written from 'within' a particular theory or perspective. This chapter explores these issues by looking at:

- longer or 'full' introductions for essays over 1,500 words;
- basic short introductions for essays under 1,500 words.

7.1   Longer or 'full' introductions

With longer essays, introductions can be written as a section in their own right and may well be several paragraphs long. 'Full' introductions generally do most or all of the following: identify the subject of the essay; signpost the shape and content of the argument; highlight the major debates that lie 'behind' the question; define terms; and (sometimes) establish a position. We will consider each of these features in more detail below.

Identifying the subject of the essay

The easiest way to do this is to refer back to the question. Let's take an example from everyday life (for examples treated in more depth, see the full essays in Chapter 13). For instance, if the essay question asks you to, 'Evaluate the claim that *Coronation Street* is the most enjoyable contemporary British soap opera', you may want to write:

> This essay will evaluate the claim that *Coronation Street* is the most enjoyable contemporary British soap opera.

However, you can always be more creative than this, provided what you write is relevant. For example, you might write:

Coronation Street consistently receives high viewer ratings. This essay explores the basis of this popularity, evaluating its appeal in comparison with *EastEnders*, one of its major ratings rivals.

Signposting the shape of the argument

The intention here is to give the reader a 'road map' of the essay. At its simplest this involves highlighting the main stages of your argument. For instance, you might write:

The first section focuses on . . . This argument is developed in the following section, which compares . . .

Identifying the sequence and shape of your argument in this manner is called 'signposting' and it is an important technique you can deploy throughout an essay.

Highlighting major debates and signposting the content of the argument

Essay questions will often centre on a key debate or debates: for example, 'Do the wealthier Western nations exploit the poorer nations?' or 'Is behaviour biologically or socially produced?' Often these debates will not be referred to explicitly but will lie 'behind' or be implied in the question. Your introduction will need to pull out these debates and signpost your essay's responses to them. This will form the core of your argument. For instance, in the *Coronation Street* example, it may be possible to argue that, historically, the show has emphasized a less naturalistic style than *EastEnders*, one characterized by strong female characters and comic men. With this in mind, it might be that one of the debates lying 'behind' the question centres on the issue of whether *Coronation Street*'s less naturalistic style is more appealing to certain audiences or whether people are more drawn to the much-vaunted 'gritty realism' of *EastEnders*. In order to refer to this debate, your introduction could be rewritten to look like this:

Coronation Street consistently receives high viewer ratings. This essay explores the basis of this popularity, evaluating its appeal in comparison with *EastEnders*, one of its major ratings rivals. In the process, the essay will analyse *Coronation Street*'s use of strong female characters, its exploration of women's lives, and its often humorous treatment of men, contrasting these to the 'gritty realism' of its competitor show.

65

You will see that this introduction not only draws attention to the possible difference in style between *Coronation Street* and *EastEnders* (a debate lying 'behind' the question), but also suggests that its appeal lies in particular features of the show: strong women characters, its exploration of women's lives and the humorous treatment of men. In other words, the introduction signposts these as central components of the essay's argument.

Defining terms

People can be over-enthusiastic about defining terms. You don't need to define absolutely everything, particularly terms that are in widespread everyday use. Nevertheless, definitions can be useful in relation to the following:

- *Key concepts and obviously technical terms*
  For example, if you are asked to assess critically a particular theory or concept (say, the notion of globalization, the cultural imperialism thesis, or cognitive developmental theory), it is fairly obvious that you will need to provide a definition or outline of it. In fact, it may be that this definition or outline will require several sentences and will look over-long and clumsy if included with your other introductory remarks. In consequence, you may decide that it is more appropriate to allot it a section of its own, perhaps immediately after the introduction proper.
- *Terms that are contested*
  For instance, the question 'Is the family in Britain in crisis?' hinges upon how you define 'crisis'. For some people factors such as the rising post-war divorce rate, increased numbers of lone-parent families and the increasing profile of feminism and lesbian and gay relationships constitute a 'crisis'. Other people find these developments positive or less problematic. Here you would need to point to the contested nature of the term and highlight the fact that it is open to competing definitions.
- *Theories or approaches that have different versions*
  Particularly on more advanced undergraduate courses where there is a greater emphasis on theoretical complexity, you will need to define the particular version of the theory or approach that you are using. For example, it may not be enough to say that you will use a perspective informed by postmodern theory or feminist theory, since there are competing versions of both. You may choose to align your argument with that of a particular theorist, or even a selected work by a particular theorist. You can do this in two main ways: naming the theorist and, more convincingly, making accurate use of the sorts of terminology he or she uses.

Establishing a position

Establishing a position means indicating the particular 'line' that you intend to take in an essay. The statement, 'This essay explores the use of capital punishment in the USA', certainly tells us what the essay is about. However, the statement, 'This essay explores the use of capital punishment in the USA and argues that it is a fundamental abuse of human rights', clearly establishes the author's position on this issue and anticipates or signals the content of the essay's conclusion. This helps orient the reader to the essay's argument and ensures that the main point is lodged in her or his mind.

What would our *Coronation Street* example look like if we included a statement that identified our position? Perhaps something like this:

> *Coronation Street* consistently receives high viewer ratings. This essay explores the basis of this popularity, evaluating its appeal in comparison with *EastEnders*, one of its major ratings rivals. In its opening section, the essay uses a feminist analysis to argue that *Coronation Street*'s appeal may be found in its 'women-centredness', in particular its focus on strong female characters, its exploration of women's lives and its often humorous treatment of men. The essay then goes on to explore the contrasting approach adopted in *EastEnders*, which has often focused on social issues and emphasized a 'gritty realism'. The essay argues that, in comparison to *Coronation Street*, this 'gritty realism' fails to connect with women's culture and that it is the appeal to women of these less naturalistic elements that underlies *Coronation Street*'s continuing popularity.

The 'position' established here is a feminist one. In other words, we are indicating that we will make a feminist reading of soap opera. A more advanced introduction might include a nod to Christine Geraghty or Charlotte Brunsdon who have written on the positive significance of soaps as feminist texts: 'In its opening section, the essay draws on Geraghty (1991) for a feminist analysis of the television programme, arguing that *Coronation Street*'s appeal may be found in its "women-centredness", in particular . . .'

An alternative structure for the full introduction

Full introductions will signpost the content of each section of the essay. A straightforward way of doing this is to list the sections in the order in which they appear, as above. Alternatively, you may wish to indicate the broad order of the essay, emphasizing the most significant arguments, but at the end of your introduction say what you will be doing next. Like this:

Coronation Street consistently receives high viewer ratings and this essay explores the basis of this popularity. The essay argues that *Coronation Street*'s appeal may be found in its 'women-centredness', in particular its focus on strong female characters, its exploration of women's lives and its often humorous treatment of men. The essay then goes on to explore the contrasting approach adopted in *EastEnders*, one of its main ratings rivals, which has often focused on social issues and emphasized a 'gritty realism'. The essay argues that, in comparison to *Coronation Street*, this 'gritty realism' fails to connect with women's culture and that it is the appeal to women of these less naturalistic elements that underlies *Coronation Street*'s continuing popularity. First, however, the essay considers Dorothy Hobson's (1982) analysis of the importance of ritual engagement with television programmes such as soap operas.

7.2 Basic short introductions

In a very short essay you may only have between 50 and 100 words to tell your reader what the essay is about. As a result, your introduction will need to be concise and highly focused. It should still:

- identify the subject of the essay and define key terms;
- highlight any major debates that lie 'behind' the question;
- signpost the essay's key argument(s).

However, it would probably stop there. Thus, a short introduction to the question, 'Evaluate the claim that *Coronation Street* is the most enjoyable contemporary British soap opera', might read more like one of our earlier versions, for example:

Coronation Street consistently receives high viewer-ratings. This essay explores the basis of this popularity, evaluating its appeal in comparison with ratings rival *EastEnders*. The essay will analyse *Coronation Street*'s use of strong female characters, its exploration of women's lives, and its often humorous treatment of men, contrasting these to the 'gritty realism' of its competitor show.

Outlining the content of your core argument will alert your reader to what is most important about the essay, or what makes it 'hang together'. You may notice that the sequence signposts have changed in this shorter version. This will not always be the case, but you may find that when you strip your work down to the bare bones, the emphasis of the argument changes, as has happened in this case.

The difference between an introductory level introduction and one that is at a more advanced level is somewhat nuanced; however, at the more advanced level, the vernacular of the field, including background themes and debates, will be skilfully deployed, while at introductory level, it is expected that introductions will be more descriptive and less steeped in the language and background of the subject area. Intermediate level essays will make proficient use of key terms, and may move towards indicating background issues and debates that will have shaped the essay question.

Turn to Essay 3, Chapter 13. This provides an example of a formal social science essay. Read the introduction and answer yes or no.

- Can you see the different elements described above?
- Has the introduction told the reader what the essay is about?
- Has it provided a synopsis of the key points?
- Has it indicated any 'underlying debates'?
- Has it indicated the structure of the essay?
- Do you think this is a good introduction?
- Could it be improved?

7.3   When do you write the introduction?

The difficulty with introduction writing is that sometimes you only know how the core arguments have developed when you have finished your essay. So, although writing the introduction can help to give you a clearer idea of what you plan to do, and in what order, you may find it is better to finalize your introduction once the rest of the essay is complete.

Summary

- Introductions tell the reader what your essay is about and give an indication of the order in which your arguments will appear.
- Introductions should normally be between 5 and 10 per cent of the total length of the essay.
- There is more than one way to write an introduction. The approach adopted here treats the introduction as an 'abstract' or synopsis of key points.

(Continued)

(Continued)

- 'Full' introductions: identify the subject of the essay; signpost the shape of the argument; highlight the major debates that lie 'behind' the question; signpost the content of the argument; (where necessary) define terms; (sometimes) establish a position or look ahead to the conclusion.
- A basic short introduction should tell the reader what the essay is about by: identifying the subject of the essay; highlighting the major debates that lie 'behind' the question; and identifying the essay's key argument(s) or theme(s).
- An introduction written to 'introductory' standards should be proficient at identifying the subject of the essay and signposting the shape of the argument.
- An introduction written to an 'intermediate' standard should move towards highlighting the major debates raised by the essay question, signposting the content of the argument, (if necessary) defining terms effectively, and (if appropriate) establishing a position.
- An introduction written to an 'advanced' standard should show greater sophistication in bringing out the major debates raised by the question, signposting the content of the argument, (if necessary) defining terms, and (if appropriate) establishing a position.
- You may write your introduction first to give you an idea of what you are doing, but you are likely to produce a better introduction once you have completed the rest of your essay.
- Essays 1 and 3 in Chapter 13 illustrate stronger introductions. Essays 2 and 4 in Chapter 13 illustrate weaker introductions.

Self-test

1 What are the components of a full introduction?
2 What is signposting and why is it important to the reader?
3 What, at minimum, should a short or basic introduction do?
4 What are some of the differences between introductory, intermediate and advanced level essays?
5 When should you write the introduction?

8

Writing the Main Section

- Structuring your argument
- Using evidence to support your argument
- Adding weight to your argument
- Communicating your argument

Before you begin drafting your main section you may find it helpful to look back at Chapter 4, particularly the guidance on how to make your main section address appropriately the type of question you are answering. You may also want to review Chapter 6, particularly the section on developing an argument.

8.1 Structuring your argument

Your essay needs a strong and coherent structure if you are to convince your reader of your case. Central to this is the process of building an argument (that is, making each point follow on from the previous one). It has been argued that creating a logical progression to a social scientific argument is not dissimilar to the way we argue in everyday life. In the example below, we imagine what may be said in a discussion about whether it is better to cook at home, or to have a meal out with friends.

'I think it is usually better to have friends round and to cook for them at home.'

'You can decide what to have on the day, and you don't have to book for a particular time. And there's no problem about transport, or parking.'

'You can dress up for spag bol if you feel like it – or have fancy food in your pyjamas if you like.'

'Most of the time, homecooked food tastes better and is better for you. I don't use any cheap "substitute" ingredients and I use a lot less salt and sugar in my recipes than they do in most restaurants. And you don't have to have standard portions – if someone wants a little or a lot, they can have a small portion or seconds.'

'Besides, I really like cooking, and I think it's nice to share new recipes with my friends.'

You might notice that this is similar to the kind of argument you would find in an advocacy essay: there isn't much scope for compare and contrast and there is little evaluation. There is a logical progression that explains the author's position. If we break it down, it looks something like this:

- *Outlines a particular point of view*
  'I think it is usually better to have friends round and to cook for them at home.'
- *Gives reasons for holding this view*
  'You can decide what to have on the day; . . . don't have to book for a particular time; . . . there's no problem about transport, or parking; . . . you can dress up . . . if you like; . . . homecooked food tastes better and is better for you; . . . you don't have to have standard portions; . . . it's nice to share new recipes with my friends.'
- *Gives evidence*
  Homecooked food and cooking for friends is better because: 'I don't use any cheap "substitute" ingredients and I use a lot less salt and sugar in my recipes than they do in most restaurants; . . . if someone wants a little or a lot, they can have a small portion or seconds.'

If you're the sort of person who likes diagrams, you can represent the stages of this process as in Figure 7.

You might suggest that there is considerable room for debate here; and you might also notice there are some implicit qualifiers throughout the argument above. For instance, problems with parking might be just as difficult near your or your friends' home as at a restaurant; and the author uses the phrases 'most of the time' and 'most restaurants', suggesting that home-cooked food isn't always better and some restaurants might use similar ingredients in their cooking. To make this a stronger argument, these debates and

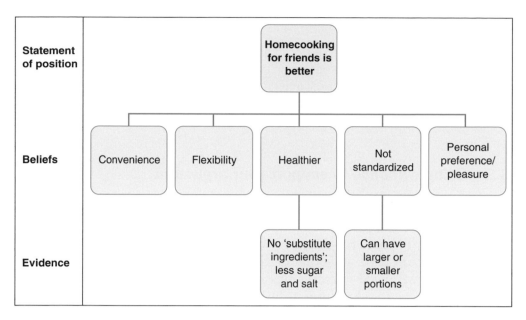

Figure 7 'Homecooking for friends versus going out to eat': logical progression arguing that homecooking is better

qualifiers would need to be addressed. To make this into an essay form, it would also, of course, need an introduction and a conclusion.

If you now turn to Essay 1 in Chapter 13, you will find a formal example of an essay that develops a logically progressing argument. What are the main stages in the essay's argument?

If we 'strip down' the argument in Essay 1, we can see that it goes through the following stages:

1 It makes the claim that a social constructionist account is more persuasive than the alternative, biological account.
2 It identifies reasons to support this view (for example, Butler's notion that sex/gender is a 'performative enactment'; Connell's argument that sex/gender is a relational category produced in a process of 'hegemonic' struggle).
3 It cites evidence from the sociological research literature on sex/gender and schooling to evaluate this argument.
4 Of course, the stages of the argument in Essay 1 are slightly more complicated than this. For instance, it uses Connell early on to question some aspects of the social constructionist case and then returns to these points in its conclusion. However, this basic structure can still be seen, as it were, beneath the surface of the essay.

Summary

- The argument in the main section of an essay needs to have a 'logical progression'.
- We construct logically progressing arguments in everyday life.
- Logical progression involves: outlining a particular point of view; giving reasons why this point of view might be correct; and providing theoretical and empirical evidence to support these claims.

8.2   Using evidence to support your argument

In Section 2.2, it was argued that claims made in social science essays need to be supported by appropriate *evidence*. Indeed, more advanced undergraduate courses are likely to require you to draw on an increasing range of sources, including primary texts and other original material. Clearly, in handling this material, you will need to reorganize it in a way that answers the question. You will also need to select from it the evidence that most effectively supports your argument.

Selecting evidence – using a range of examples

Any essay question will expect you to support your arguments with appropriate examples and evidence. However, as you develop intermediate and advanced essay writing skills, you will be expected to demonstrate an increasing ability to select examples that illustrate and support your points most effectively.

In general, you should:

- *Highlight examples that have the most significant or far-reaching implications.* The examples will need to be relevant to the question and engage with the point that you are making. This means being selective. You cannot cite every single related example or piece of evidence in the relevant literature. Some examples will be more useful to your purpose than others, and you will need to identify these and relate them to the issue under discussion.
- *Where possible, support your argument with more than one example.* This does not mean that you should use a number of examples to make the same point over and over again. Rather, what is being suggested is that you will need to draw on a range of examples to illustrate the different aspects of your argument. However, you will sometimes need to decide whether it is more effective to explore an issue in depth or in breadth. For instance, exploring one or a limited range of examples in depth may allow you to provide a richer and more detailed account than exploring a breadth of examples only briefly. You

will need to decide which strategy is most appropriate according to the question and the material available.

- *Select examples from a range of sources.*
  Particularly on more advanced undergraduate courses, you will need to look for a breadth of source material, thereby demonstrating your familiarity with the field. As well as the academic literature, it may be that up-to-the-minute examples can be found in, for example, news and current affairs. Where such examples are effective in illuminating an academic argument they can be a useful addition to your essay.
- *Work from the general to the particular.*
  Specific examples should be used to support general arguments. Whereas a general argument cannot necessarily be induced from only one or two concrete examples, one or two concrete examples can be used to illustrate the plausibility of a general argument on the grounds that there are many more examples of the same point but, due to the limits of the word count and because you don't wish to be repetitive, it is not possible to cite them in your essay.

Turn to Essay 1 in Chapter 13. What examples can you identify and how are these used?

As you will have seen, Essay 1 cites a range of examples from the research literature on sex/gender and schooling to support and illustrate what it identifies as the three major arguments to be found in this literature (that the content and practices of schooling encode sex/gender; that pupils actively use sex/gender to negotiate schooling; and that sex/gender relations intersect with other social relations in the school). It attempts to identify particularly 'rich' examples, to cite different sources, to indicate where similar data can be found in other research, and to work from the general to the particular.

Selecting evidence – using empirical evidence

In the preceding paragraphs we have explored, in general terms, the use of examples as evidence. However, it is important to be clear that these examples will frequently be drawn from concrete research findings. Social scientists carry out research studies to gather evidence to substantiate or falsify their theories and arguments. Evidence from such research is called empirical evidence (loosely speaking, evidence collected via systematic and rigorous observation), and since it comes from checkable, usually published investigation, it is more highly regarded than everyday examples or personal experience. As is the case with Essay 1, a good essay will use empirical evidence to support the arguments made. This involves more than simply describing relevant research findings. The task is to make clear exactly how these findings support or illustrate your arguments. For example, if you look at Essay 1 you will find the following paragraph:

> As well as producing sex/gender through friendship group inter-actions, the literature also suggests that pupils use sex/gender to negotiate and resist schooling. Kehily and Nayak (1996, p. 214) describe an account from a group of secondary school pupils in which one of them (Samantha) was claimed to have pursued a teacher (Mr Smedley) round the classroom with a sprig of mistletoe with the intention of 'getting some lipstick on the top of his head'. In this instance, a hetero-sexualized form of femininity is used satirically to undermine the authority of a male teacher (see also Walkerdine, 1981).

This paragraph:

- identifies the argument (that the social meanings and practices of sex/gender are used by pupils to negotiate and resist schooling);
- cites research evidence to support this claim (from Kehily and Nayak, 1996);
- explains exactly how this evidence illustrates the initial argument (it is an instance where heterosexual femininity was used to undermine a male teacher's authority); and
- provides an additional reference identifying further research findings supporting this argument (Walkerdine, 1981).

Selecting evidence – using maps, diagrams and numerical data

Maps, diagrams and numerical data are further major sources of evidence that you can use to illustrate and support your argument. Rather like quotations, maps, diagrams and numerical data should be used to illustrate and support points in your argument and not to replace it, so always remember to integrate them into the points you are making. In addition, remember that maps, tables and graphs are not hard facts. You will need to be critical of your numerical sources by, for example, bearing in mind what scale is being used and how this shapes the evidence, by questioning how data have been collected, or by asking how a graph would change if plotted over a wider timescale. You should also be aware that numerical data represent specific outcomes and that the underlying causes of those outcomes will be unclear and will need further investigation. For example, it is quite possible for different combinations of causes to produce a similar numerical outcome.

Have a look at Figure 8.

In this case, the data is from the UK's Office of National Statistics, which is generally considered to be a reliable source. However, we might want to

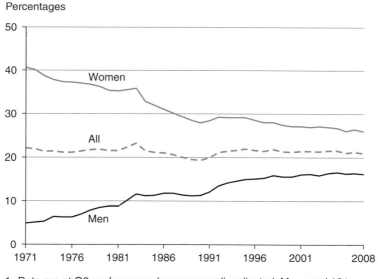

United Kingdom

Percentages

1 Data are at Q2 each year and are seasonally adjusted. Men aged 16 to
   64 and women aged 16 to 59. See Appendix, Part 4: Labour Force Survey.

Figure 8 Economic inactivity rates:[1] by sex

Source: Labour Force Survey, Office for National Statistics, Social Trends 39, Figure 4.18, p.58

know how 'economic inactivity' is defined (in fact the ONS does this in its glossary, www.statistics.gov.uk/downloads/theme_social/Social_Trends39/ Social_Trends_39.pdf, p. 61) and whether the data came from self-reporting or population studies of employment. The timescale here is relatively long, but might show a different picture if we had data from the 1950s – or if the data were divided not just by gender, but also by class or educational attainment. In reading the data, of course, we need to be careful not to infer causation from correlation. In other words, it might appear that *because* women's economic activity has increased, men's has decreased. However, we have correlation here, but not cause. From this data, it is impossible to say why women's economic inactivity has decreased, nor why men's has increased, just that it has.

Also, data may appear to tell a different story depending on the form that they come in. For instance, compare the table and chart below. Which is 'easier' to understand? Which tells the clearer, or fuller, story?

If you reproduce or copy sections or selections from maps, diagrams or numerical data as we have here, you will need to give your sources for them. However, it is often sufficient to refer to them, for example, by saying 'As the data used by Smith show . . . (Smith, 2005, p. 15, Table 1)', and providing a full reference at the end of your essay (references are dealt with in detail in Chapter 10).

Table 1 Reasons for economic inactivity: by sex and age, 2008

United Kingdom					Percentages
	16–24	25–34	35–49	50–59/64	All aged 16–59/64
Men					
Long-term sick or disabled	5	40	62	49	34
Looking after family or home	1	9	16	6	6
Student	82	27	4	–	33
Retired	0	0	1	33	13
Other	10	17	12	9	11
All men (=100%) (millions)[1]	1.2	0.3	0.5	1.3	3.3
Women					
Long-term sick or disabled	3	8	24	41	19
Looking after family or home	23	72	61	27	45
Student	66	10	4	1	22
Retired	0	0	–	14	3
Other	8	8	8	14	9
All women (=100%) (millions)[1]	1.3	0.9	1.4	1.1	4.7

1 Includes discouraged workers and those who are temporarily sick.

Source: Labour Force Survey, Office for National Statistics, Social Trends 39, Figure 4.20, p.59

http://www.statistics.gov.uk/downloads/theme_social/Social_Trends39/Social_Trends_39.pdf (accessed 7 July 2010)

Using theory, being 'critical'

Essay questions will often require you to explore theoretical arguments as well as concrete examples, and you will also want to draw on other people's theories as evidence to support your own argument. The ability to demonstrate an understanding of competing theoretical positions and to identify the fundamental strengths and weaknesses of each is a basic requirement of undergraduate essay writing. As you develop intermediate and advanced essay writing skills you will be expected to demonstrate the ability to understand and apply arguments from primary theoretical texts (as opposed to relying on commentaries on these), demonstrate an understanding of more complex theoretical positions, be more confident in expressing a reasoned preference for one theoretical position over another; and demonstrate the ability to write from 'within' a perspective or theory.

In working with theories remember that this is like looking through different pairs of spectacles – they make us see the world in different ways, such as in a poststructuralist way or in a feminist way. As a result, we have to accept that theories do not let us see the world 'as it is'; we see only what they allow us to see. In fact, as we saw in Section 2.2, many social scientists argue that we can never see the world 'as it is' and that we always have to look at

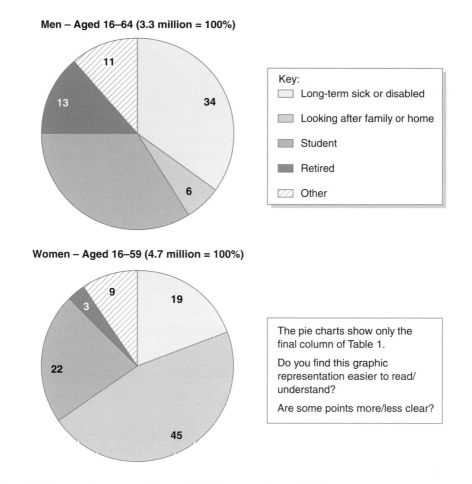

Men – Aged 16–64 (3.3 million = 100%)

Key:
- [ ] Long-term sick or disabled
- [ ] Looking after family or home
- [ ] Student
- [ ] Retired
- [/] Other

34, 6, 13, 11

Women – Aged 16–59 (4.7 million = 100%)

19, 45, 22, 3, 9

The pie charts show only the final column of Table 1.

Do you find this graphic representation easier to read/ understand?

Are some points more/less clear?

Figure 9 Reasons for economic inactivity: by sex and age, 2008

Source: Adapted from Labour Force Survey, Office for National Statistics, 'Reasons for economic inactivity', Social Trends 39, Figure 4.20, p.59. http://www.statistics.gov.uk/downloads/theme_social/Social_Trends39/ Social_Trends_39.pdf (accessed 7 July 2010)

it from one perspective or another. The task is to find a 'pair of spectacles' that allows us to view the object under study in as useful a way as possible. These points have some important implications:

- Competing theories are not all equal. Different theories appeal to different kinds of evidence. Different theories are 'useful' in different contexts.
- You cannot lump together the good bits of a whole range of theories to make one 'super-theory'. Different theories will contradict each other. As a result, incorporating an insight from one theory into an existing approach will often require a radical restructuring of both.

- Even when you can make a new theory from aspects of previous ones, you still won't have a view of the world 'as it really is'. You may have a more powerful pair of spectacles to look through but you will still have to ask yourself the following questions: Is there something beyond the range of these spectacles that I can't see? Are these spectacles still obscuring what I can see? If I turn to look at a new object, do my spectacles work as well as they did when I looked at the first object? Asking these sorts of questions is called being 'critical'. This doesn't mean being negative about everything. It means 'standing outside' a theory, looking for its limitations as well as its strengths.

Essay 1 provides a formal example of an essay that demonstrates a systematic engagement with and evaluation of theoretical material. You may want to look, in particular, at the conclusion, where the author attempts to identify some of the limitations of the theoretical arguments in the literature on sex/gender and schooling. You may also want to compare the use of theoretical material in Essay 1 with that in Essay 2. Turn to Essays 1 and 2 in Chapter 13. In what ways is Essay 1 more effective in handling and applying theory? You may now wish also to read the tutor comments following each essay.

Writing from 'within' a theory or perspective

At several points in the previous chapters the importance of writing from 'within' a theory or perspective has been highlighted, particularly in the context of more advanced undergraduate and postgraduate courses. This refers to the ability to take on the conceptual world-view of a particular theoretical standpoint. Individual social scientists are generally identified as working within and contributing to particular theoretical traditions. For example, the work of Stuart Hall, Emeritus Professor of Sociology at the Open University, has been closely identified with a culturalist and poststructuralist rereading of the Italian Marxist, Antonio Gramsci. The work of Margaret Wetherell, Professor in Social Psychology at the Open University, is closely identified with a discursive approach to psychology. Like other social scientists, both Hall and Wetherell can be said to write from 'within' the conceptual universe of these specific perspectives. Their work is steeped in the histories of these perspectives; it reproduces and clarifies the perspectives' distinctive vocabularies and conceptual tools, and contributes to knowledge through applying these tools to new objects of enquiry and by questioning and pushing at the boundaries of their respective traditions.

The ability to write from within a perspective or theory can, then, be said to have at least two important aspects. First, it is a sign of increasing intellectual maturity. It demonstrates a familiarity with, and confidence in handling, the vocabulary and conceptual framework of a particular theoretical tradition. Second, it demonstrates the confidence to take sides in intellectual debates. The social scientist's duty to evaluate critically does not mean that we should adopt a uniform and bland relativism where all forms of knowledge are considered equally useful. The point of writing from 'within' a particular perspective or theory is that you are prepared to take a stand and say, 'This is useful knowledge'. This does not mean that you should attempt to shape evidence to fit a preconceived standpoint. It means taking an informed position on the basis of reasoned academic judgement and with due reference to the potential limits of your own arguments. An example of a student essay in which the author clearly writes from 'within' a perspective (social constructionism) and uses this to take up a firm position on the set question can be found in Essay 1 in Chapter 13.

However, it is worth stressing that essay questions will not of necessity require that you write from 'within' a perspective or theory. Indeed, they may specify that you should adopt an explicitly neutral position, standing 'outside' one or more positions in order to evaluate them critically. You may now wish to read Essay 3 in Chapter 13. Essay 3 attempts to develop an objective viewpoint, but is ultimately critical of the arguments of theorist Manuel Castells. This essay engages with different concepts and theoretical positions, but would you say it is written 'within a perspective'?

Importantly, keep in mind that it will not always be possible to make a reasoned judgement between competing positions. After careful consideration, you may decide that the explanations they offer are equally strong or equally weak. If this is the case, you should say so.

Being 'self-reflexive'

In the social sciences, choosing between competing theories or arguments will, at some point, involve making a value judgement. Although it may be possible to identify clear reasons why some arguments are more persuasive than others, our choice will almost inevitably be shaped by our political, moral and philosophical values. While not all social scientific writing will demonstrate this, it is good practice to make explicit the theoretical or political orientation that underpins your work rather than pretending that your argument is simply 'objective'. For example, you might indicate that the essay is being written from 'within' a feminist, or Foucauldian, or cognitive development perspective. This will alert readers to possible bias or areas of partiality in your argument and will allow them to make up their own minds about the strengths of your case. In fact, by signalling your possible blind spots to the reader, you are being more objective than if you pretended such blind spots did not exist.

For example, in Essay 1 in Chapter 13 the author clearly indicates in the introduction that, on the basis of reasoned judgement, the essay is written from a position sympathetic to a particular theory ('social constructionism'). This alerts the reader to the potential bias in the subsequent material.

Summary

- As you progress to more advanced undergraduate courses you will increasingly be required to select relevant material from a range of sources and relate this back to the individual essay question.
- Arguments should be supported with appropriate illustrations and evidence. Try to select a range of the most significant examples – some are richer and more far-reaching than others. Examples should relate back to the essay question and engage with the argument that you are making.
- For some courses you will need to use maps, diagrams or numerical data. These should be used as evidence to support your argument, but remember, they are not 'hard facts'.
- Social science essays often ask you to explore theoretical arguments and use these as evidence as well as concrete examples. As you develop your essay writing skills you will need to show increasing confidence in exploring the strengths and weaknesses of competing theories.
- Some theories are stronger and more convincing than others; theories cannot necessarily be lumped together to make a 'super-theory' – they often contradict each other. In handling theories, social scientists need to be 'critical', that is, they need to display an awareness of a theory's weaknesses and its strengths. However, one sign of increasing intellectual maturity is the ability to write from 'within' a perspective.
- Being 'self-reflexive' means acknowledging your own particular biases, for example, by indicating that you are arguing from a specific point of view.
- Many of these points are illustrated in Essays 1 and 3 in Chapter 13.

8.3 Adding weight to your argument

Social scientists highlight key works and use quotations for the following reasons:

- as a source of evidence, that is, to support and illustrate their own points;
- to provide the reader with a 'map' of the most important work done in the area under discussion;
- to demonstrate to the reader that they have thought about and understood what other people have written on a subject and that their own arguments should be taken seriously.

As you progress to intermediate and more advanced undergraduate courses you should expect to demonstrate an increased ability to select appropriate quotations and cite key texts in order to add weight to your argument.

Let's take a brief look at some examples of these strategies in operation. In the following, John Urry describes the historically exceptional use of oil and petroleum products in a discussion of the impact of capitalist systems and excessive consumption on global climate change.

> (T)he peaking of oil supplies occurred in the US as far back as 1971 and oil production worldwide is now probably peaking. This is because new oil fields, and especially giant fields, have not been discovered at the same rate as they were discovered during most of the 20th century (Heinberg, 2005; Homer-Dixon, 2006, ch. 4; Rifkin, 2002, ch. 2; but see P. Jackson, 2006). Energy is thus increasingly expensive and there will be frequent shortages. This is especially so with the world's population continuing to increase in size, its profligate consumption of oil . . ., and its exceptional rate of current and future urbanization. There is not enough oil to fuel such worldwide energy systems, with experts estimating that global consumption would, with business as usual, double by 2050 (Homer-Dixon, 2006: 174).
>
> (Urry, 2010, p. 196)

Urry makes a series of claims here. The first is that 'oil production . . . is . . . peaking'. This is supported – or authority added to this claim – by citing three authors who agree, and one, Peter Jackson, who has a slightly different 'take' on 'peak oil' (though we don't from this sentence know what that take is). Urry then argues that the cost of energy is increasing and that there is not enough to go round. Moreover, he suggests that the problem is going to get worse due to human population growth, inefficient use of oil and increased urbanization. Finally, he supports the claim that things are getting worse by citing Homer-Dixon, who has convinced Urry that if we continue current consumption levels, increase urbanization and global human population, oil use will 'double by 2050'. Urry has accomplished two things with these citations. The first is that he has progressed his argument, lending weight to his claims by citing a range of experts or authorities; the second is that he has indicated the field on which he is drawing – demonstrating that there are a number of authors who are taking the issue of peak oil seriously.

In the next passage, Urry uses two quotations to support his argument, one short and one long:

> Rifkin claims that the oil age is 'winding down as fast as it revved up' (2002: 174). . . . [T]he Transition Towns movement . . . well captures the . . . global significance of what some call the 'petroleum interval' in human

history, a brief century or so . . . between oil's first discovery in 1859 and its demise in the early years of this century (Hopkins, 2008: 20–1). Kunstler considers the systems effects of such peaking:

> At peak and just beyond, there is massive potential for system failures of all kinds, social, economic, and political. Peak is quite literally a tipping point. Beyond peak, things unravel and the center does not hold. Beyond peak, all bets are off about civilization's future. (2006: 65; see also Homer-Dixon, 2006)

(Urry, 2010, p. 196)

There are several points that are worth pulling out of these examples:

- In each case, the writer uses his quotations or citations of other authors to support a point that he himself is making. This is important because there is a temptation to let quotations in particular do the work for you. Quotations and references to other people's work should support rather than replace your argument.
- In the case of the direct quotations, Urry has chosen them because they are pithy – or succinctly express a point in a way Urry finds particularly compelling.
- Urry makes certain he introduces the quotations with a clear indication of who is 'speaking': 'Rifkin claims that . . .' and 'Kunstler considers the . . .'. Quotations that are not introduced in some way can sometimes read as if they have appeared out of nowhere and interrupt the 'flow' of the writing.
- In the case of the first quotation, it is enclosed in single inverted commas – or quotation marks – and falls within the line of the sentence. Short quotes, of up to about 30 words or two lines, are usually included in the main sentence. It is usual to indent longer quotations on the left margin (and sometimes the right as well), to distinguish them from your own argument. The second quotation is separate from the sentence introduction and is indented, without inverted commas.
- Shortening or adding to your quoted material needs to be shown. If you leave out phrases or sentences, indicate such cuts with three dots (. . .), known as an ellipsis. Similarly, if you need to add or substitute a word, letter or phrase to clarify the sense, put your inserted words in square brackets. For example, '. . . [T]he Transition Towns movement . . .' shows that we have cut the sentence prior to the word 'the' – and because we have lost part of that sentence we have now had to add a capital letter to the word '[T]he' that did not appear in the original.
- Urry is very careful to provide references for the work cited. He has used a version of the Harvard referencing system (this is explained in detail in Chapter 10) but there are other systems, including footnote or endnote systems that may be preferred by your tutor or university.

Summary

- As your skills develop, and certainly at intermediate and advanced standards, you should be able to select appropriate quotations and cite key texts in support of your argument.
- Quotations and references to key texts are used: as a source of evidence; to provide the reader with a 'map' of the most important works in an area; and to give the work 'authority'.
- Quotations should be introduced.
- Shorter quotations can be written in the main text in single inverted commas. Longer quotations should be written in a separate paragraph indented at the left-hand (and sometimes right-hand) margins. Any changes should be indicated.
- Quotations and key texts highlighted in an essay must be supported by a reference, in the style preferred by your tutor or university.

8.4   Communicating your argument

You may feel happy that you have grasped the essay question and are able to answer it comprehensively and logically, but to prove this you will need to be able to convey your ideas, to communicate them to your reader.

Thinking about the audience

Students often ask who their reader is meant to be. Commonly, this reader is identified as the 'intelligent layperson'. While this notion is useful, it presents problems in that even the intelligent layperson cannot be expected to know much of the technical vocabulary that is taken for granted in the social sciences. Perhaps a more useful idea is to think of your reader as someone studying the social sciences at the same level as you but at another university. You can assume that your reader will have a grasp of basic social scientific ideas, so you won't need to explain every last detail to them. However, they won't necessarily be studying the same things as you, so you will need to explain more complex ideas and be careful to define your terms. For the most advanced undergraduate courses you can assume that your reader will have a greater degree of sophistication and you can therefore afford to write with more complexity. In fact, by the end of advanced undergraduate courses you should probably aim to be writing for an expert audience.

Clear sentences and paragraphs

The general rule in essay writing is to keep your sentences simple and easily understood. However, like other academic fields, the social sciences tend to have formal written styles and specialized vocabularies. Social scientific vocabulary cannot be dismissed simply as 'jargon' (although sometimes this might be a justified criticism). Academic disciplines need a complex language to be able to deal with complex issues. Unfortunately, this may cause you problems. There is a real danger that in trying to sound 'academic' you may simply sound confused. The best advice is probably to say that, if you are unsure, use the language that you understand. Even when you feel more confident you need to remember that there is nothing to be gained from using complex language for its own sake. The real test lies in being able to communicate complex ideas in the form that is most easily understood.

Equally, your paragraphs need to be as clear and straightforward as possible. The 'Rubin method' of paragraph analysis (Rubin, 1983) suggests that paragraphs have:

- a topic;
- a series of statements that explain what the author thinks is special or relevant about the topic; and that, put together, these form the paragraph's
- main idea.

There is a general rule that essays have three main ideas or arguments, with each idea having a set of supporting paragraphs and sub-points. Depending on the question, however, a 1,500-word essay may have five or six key points as well as an introduction and conclusion. Each paragraph should address one key point or one aspect of a key point.

Look again at the Urry examples in Section 8.3. Using the Rubin method, can you discern the 'main idea' in each?

For the first paragraph, we have talked through the series of statements (or claims) and identified the topic (above). The main idea can be derived from these. We might summarise that Urry argues that there is a critical convergence of high demand and reduction of supply. This leads us to the next section.

Try the Rubin method, remembering that the long and short quotes form part of Urry's argument. In short, Urry is indicating that the period of heavy oil use is something of an historical blip: current systems are going to be under increasing pressure, and alternatives, such as those explored by the Transition Town movement, are going to be needed.

Giving the essay direction

If readers are to avoid getting lost in your argument you need to tell them what is happening at key points along the way. There are three effective ways to do this:

- introduce and summarize the main sections;
- recap and signpost your argument;
- where useful, remind the reader of the subject of your essay.

These points are elaborated below but you can also see them applied in an actual essay in Essays 1 and 3 in Chapter 13.

Introducing and summarizing the main sections

To illustrate this point, here is an example from a chapter in which the author, Geoff Andrews, explores the history of political dissent in the UK and the ways in which dissent works as a set of 'living ideas'. He writes:

> The discussion in the previous section focused on the ways in which ideas of dissent were articulated in a particular historical context and some of the impacts that they had – both for the lives of the dissidents, but also crucially for . . . political rulers . . . . Therefore, from this example, we can say that dissent was a type of political participation which questioned the 'legitimacy' of the political system, its institutions, laws and policies, but also its dominant values. . . .
>
> It is important to recognize how, in this case, dissent worked as a set of living ideas. The writings of intellectuals, the language of a popular pamphlet, the force of sermons and the discussions in the coffee houses helped produce a critique of the way politics was conducted and power was distributed. In this respect the impact of dissent as a set of living ideas is clear. . . .
>
> However, there is a second way in which dissent worked as a set of living ideas at this time. The ideas of thinkers such as Godwin, Paine and Wollstonecraft were also to become part of a wider chain of ideas that developed into political ideologies. . . .
>
> (Andrews, 2005, pp. 82–3)

If we break down this passage we can see Andrews doing the following:

- He first reiterates the key point from his previous section ('the ways in which ideas of dissent were articulated in a particular historical context and some of the impacts that they had'), thus underscoring and concluding the argument of this particular section.
- Next, he reminds the reader of one of the overarching ideas running through his argument as a whole ('It is important to recognize how, in this case, dissent worked as a set of living ideas'). This creates a 'bridge' between his previous point and the one he is about to make.
- He then introduces his new point ('However, there is a second way in which dissent worked as a set of living ideas at this time') before signposting the focus of this (dissenting thought 'developed into political ideologies').

Recapping and signposting

Throughout his chapter, Andrews carefully recaps and signposts his argument as a means of binding the argument together. One frequently used device for signposting in academic writing is to indicate that there are various issues you aim to explore and then to list these as you discuss them. For instance, later in his discussion of political dissent, Andrews writes:

> The remainder of this section will expand on these three liberal justifications for the rights of dissidents . . . . First, the liberal emphasis on liberty as the core principle was on the basis that liberals should be left to their own choices. They know their own interests best, and it is not the business of the state (or any other 'collective body') to interfere with freedom of thought or expression . . .
>
> This view introduces the second liberal defence of dissent, which is that it was essential to progress. This position was apparent in Godwin's belief that the spirit of free enquiry would ultimately win out over ignorance and would be reflected in increasingly harmonious ways of living . . .
>
> Third, liberals have justified dissent on democratic-pluralist grounds. In modern liberal democratic societies, where individuals are equal before the law . . . dissent is an essential part of the political process.
>
> (Andrews, 2005, pp. 87–8)

Although there isn't the space to include the full details of Andrews' argument, you can see from the above extract how he first signposts ('The remainder of this section will expand on these three liberal justifications . . .') and then identifies the three points being made ('This view introduces the second liberal defence of dissent'). This strategy is an important means by which he helps us as readers locate ourselves within his ongoing discussion.

Having carefully developed his argument in this section of the chapter, Andrews then brings it to a close by recapping its core points. Because the chapter was written as a teaching text, Andrews does this in the form of a bullet-pointed list. This would be unusual in a formal social sciences essay where the expectation would usually be for arguments to be made using conventional paragraphs. If his summary had been written in this form it might have looked something like this:

> As the above points suggest, dissent occupies an important position in liberal theory. For liberal theory, dissent provides the opportunity for free expression, pluralism and progress.
>
> (Adapted from Andrews, 2005, p. 90)

As with his use of signposting, the careful manner in which Andrews recaps the major points in his argument underlines these and helps the reader to orient her or himself within it.

Referring back to the subject or task of the essay

Referring back to the subject or task of the essay involves reminding the reader of your main topic, arguments or themes, or the task you are undertaking. It is another way in which writers help to focus readers' attention and thus orient them within the argument. An obvious way to do this is, at strategic moments, to repeat the essay title. However, this can sometimes be clumsy or repetitious. You don't want your essay overburdened with phrases such as, 'In answering the question, "Evaluate the importance of the unconscious in Freud's theory of the mind" it is thus necessary to . . .' This is why referring back to the subject or task of the essay is perhaps best achieved by having a strong sense of these in your own mind. For instance, in one of the extracts explored above, we noted that Andrews drew attention to an overarching point in his argument (dissent as a 'living idea') when making a 'bridge' between one section and the next. In other words, Andrews' task in this section of his chapter was to convey the notion of dissent as a living idea and, in summarizing this section and introducing the next one, he carefully related the argument back to this task ('It is important to recognize how, in this case, dissent worked as a set of living ideas . . .').

Making your essay 'flow'

Link or 'transition' words, phrases and sentences are used to make an essay 'flow', that is, they make the writing easy to read by relating sentences, parts of sentences and paragraphs to each other. We can illustrate this by taking a final look at an extract from Andrews' chapter on political dissent:

> A further question worth posing here is whether dissent can take violent forms. Is terrorism a form of dissent, for example? There is no easy answer to this. Many political theorists and writers would add the qualification of 'legitimate' or 'illegitimate' dissent. That is, dissent expressed in liberal democratic societies is only legitimate if it does not resort to violence. Yet this seems to take us only part of the way. For example, deciding what is legitimate or illegitimate dissent will depend to some extent on ideological assumptions, cultural influences and political tradition. Meanings can also change over time, suggesting that one person's freedom fighter is another person's terrorist. This was the case with the African National Congress (ANC) for example, described by many opponents (including the Thatcher governments in the UK in the 1980s) as 'terrorist' because of its commitment to armed struggle. Yet following the release of Nelson Mandela in 1989 and the participation in the new post-apartheid South African government in the 1990s, this description was changed and the ANC became regarded as a mainstream political organization.
>
> (Andrews, 2005, p. 74)

Now reread the extract with many of the link words and phrases removed.

A further question worth posing here is whether dissent can take violent forms. Is terrorism a form of dissent? There is no easy answer. Many political theorists and writers would add the qualification of 'legitimate' or 'illegitimate' dissent. Dissent expressed in liberal democratic societies is only legitimate if it does not resort to violence. This seems to take us only part of the way. Deciding what is legitimate or illegitimate dissent will depend to some extent on ideological assumptions, cultural influences and political tradition. Meanings can change over time, suggesting that one person's freedom fighter is another person's terrorist. The African National Congress (ANC) was described by many opponents (including the Thatcher governments in the UK in the 1980s) as 'terrorist' because of its commitment to armed struggle. Following the release of Nelson Mandela in 1989 and the participation in the new post-apartheid South African government in the 1990s, this description was changed. The ANC became regarded as a mainstream political organization.

(Adapted from Andrews, 2005, p. 74)

Although some of the phrasing in this revised paragraph might seem punchier, much of the extract now reads like a list of unrelated points or something written in note form. In consequence, the reader is jolted from one sentence to another. In making sure you link sentences, parts of sentences and paragraphs, you ensure your reader's attention sticks to the argument and does not become distracted by your writing.

Summary

- One way to think of your notional reader is as someone studying the social sciences at an equivalent level in another university. She or he will understand basic social scientific concepts but won't necessarily be familiar with the area addressed in your essay. By the end of advanced undergraduate courses you should aim to write for an 'expert' audience.
- The aim of good essay writing is to convey complex ideas in as clear a form as possible.
- Paragraphs contain a topic and a series of statements explaining what is relevant about this topic. Together these make up its 'main idea'. A standard structure for an essay is an introduction, three main arguments or discussion points and a conclusion. However, depending on the essay question, a 1,500-word essay may have five or six key points plus an introduction and conclusion.

- You can give your essay a strong sense of direction by: introducing and summarizing main sections; recapping and signposting your argument; where useful, referring back to the question.
- Using link words and sentences ensures that your essay 'flows' smoothly.
- You can see these points applied to an actual essay in Essays 1 and 3 in Chapter 13.

Self-test

1 What are the three main stages in setting out an argument?
2 What does it mean to work 'from the general to the particular'?
3 What does it mean to write from 'within a theory or perspective'?
4 How do social scientists add 'authority' to their claims?
5 What is the Rubin method?
6 There are three main ways to give your essay direction. What are they?
7 What is the role of link or transition words and phrases?

9

Writing Conclusions

- What a conclusion should aim to do
- What a conclusion should contain

Conclusions are an important part of an essay, and a well-written conclusion is a good way of picking up extra marks.

9.1 What a conclusion should aim to do – and should not do

The primary job of a conclusion is to provide a final condensed version of the essay's core argument and in the process to provide an overview of the state of 'current knowledge' or 'current opinion' on the given topic. Since your conclusion should take up no more than 10 per cent of your essay, a short essay (of up to 1,500 words) won't have room to do much more than this. However, if you are writing a longer essay your conclusion should do the following:

- recap the key points in your argument/summarize the key debates raised by the question, and try to synthesize them;
- provide a final condensed version of the essay's core argument that restates your position on the question;
- if necessary, identify absences in your argument that could be explored in future work.

Put simply, a conclusion should leave the reader with a clear impression of your argument – what it was about, what you believe, and why you believe this. An introductory level essay is likely to demonstrate the ability to summarize content clearly and concisely. More advanced essays will be expected to progress towards writing more complex conclusions that emphasize condensed versions of your core argument.

One thing that a conclusion should not do is bring in any new material or new ideas or arguments. Some students have a tendency to 'tack on' points that they forgot to mention or didn't have space for in the main part of their essay. However, effectively saying 'And another thing!' will not gain marks and may suggest to your tutor that your essay wasn't as well planned, or your ideas as well developed, as they might have been. For an example of how easy it is to make this sort of mistake, have a look at Essay 4 in Chapter 13.

9.2   What a conclusion should contain

If you have read the chapter on writing introductions, you will remember the following question and introduction:

> 'Evaluate the claim that *Coronation Street* is the most enjoyable contemporary British soap opera.'

> *Coronation Street* consistently receives high viewer ratings. This essay explores the basis of this popularity, evaluating its appeal in comparison with *EastEnders*, one of its major ratings rivals. In its opening section, the essay uses a feminist analysis to argue that *Coronation Street*'s appeal may be found in its 'women-centredness', in particular its focus on strong female characters, its exploration of women's lives and its often humorous treatment of men. The essay then goes on to explore the contrasting approach adopted in *EastEnders*, which has often focused on social issues and emphasized a 'gritty realism'. The essay argues that, in comparison to *Coronation Street*, this 'gritty realism' fails to connect with women's culture and that it is the appeal to women of these less naturalistic elements that underlies *Coronation Street*'s continuing popularity.

Imagine that we now have to write a conclusion to the same essay. We will have written a main section that develops these arguments and provides supporting evidence to back up and illustrate our claims. We now have to bring the essay to a close, leaving the reader with a clear overall impression of our argument and our reasons for holding this position. From the introduction it's clear that the main thrust of our argument is that *Coronation Street*'s appeal lies in the way it speaks to women about their experiences and women's culture. As a result, we may well write a conclusion that looks something like the following:

> This essay has argued that, historically, *EastEnders* has adopted broadly 'realist' genre conventions. It has, for example, emphasized social diversity (witness the presence of gay characters and – in however limited a fashion – characters from black and minority ethnic groups). Similarly, it has sought to address 'difficult' social issues such as HIV infection and unemployment. In contrast, despite covering some of the same territory, *Coronation Street* has tended to adopt a more diluted naturalism. In particular, in preference to *EastEnders*' 'gritty realism', it has tended to emphasize strong female characters and has portrayed a rich array of comic situations, events and individuals, frequently at the expense of men. As the essay has suggested, it is possible to argue that these aspects of *Coronation Street* connect with the everyday cultures of its female audience and that the programme's women-centredness is central to its continuing strong position in the television ratings war.

If we break down this conclusion into its component parts, we can see that it does the following:

- recaps the key stages in the argument and summarizes the key debates raised by the question (that is, the argument that *EastEnders* favours 'gritty realism' while *Coronation Street* is less naturalistic but more women-centred);
- provides a final condensed statement of the essay's core argument (this women-centredness underlies its popular appeal).

This conclusion hasn't identified absences in the argument that could be explored in future work, and it isn't always necessary to do this. However, what if in the main section of the essay we had provided examples illustrating *Coronation Street*'s putative 'woman-centredness', but had not established (via audience research) that this was what actually appealed to women viewers? In this case, our conclusion might suggest that further research was necessary to substantiate (or falsify) our hypothesis. This, then, is an absence in our argument that could be explored in future work.

The above is one conclusion that we might have written to this particular essay question. However, you might disagree with the argument and want to write something completely different. Equally, you could have expressed the same points in a number of different ways. Alternatively, you might feel that you couldn't write a conclusion like this because it is 'too complicated' or 'too well written'. If this is the case, don't worry. You could write a serviceable conclusion in a much simpler form. The point is that there is more than one way to write a conclusion, and you should not view this example as a template to be followed slavishly.

If you want to look at more formal examples of social science essay conclusions, you should read Essays 1 and 3 in Chapter 13. In both cases the author summarizes the argument, while also taking a clear stand in relation to the question. Essay 1 also indicates some possible limitations in the literature. Compare this to the conclusions of Essays 2 and 4. Why are the conclusions to Essays 1 and 3 more successful?

Summary

- The primary job of a conclusion is to provide a final condensed version of your essay's core argument and thereby to summarize the key debates raised by the question, or provide an overview of 'current knowledge' on a given topic.
- The conclusion should not contain any new material.
- The conclusion should take up roughly 10 per cent of an essay.
- Longer conclusions should: recap the subject of the essay in some form; recap the key stages in the argument/summarize the key debates raised by the question; provide a final condensed version of the argument that restates the essay's position on the question; (if necessary) identify absences in the argument that could be explored in future work.
- An essay written to an 'introductory' standard might be expected to provide a conclusion that demonstrates an ability to summarize the content of the essay clearly and concisely. More advanced essays should move towards conclusions that emphasize sophisticated condensed versions of the core argument, and a sophisticated understanding of the key debates raised by the question.
- Examples of formal essay conclusions are available in Chapter 13.

Self-test

1 What is the purpose of a conclusion?
2 What should a conclusion *not* contain?
3 What might distinguish a conclusion written to an introductory standard from one written to an advanced standard?

10

Referencing

- What is a reference?
- Why are references needed?
- What should be referenced?
- Basic principles
- Advanced referencing
- Compiling your references

10.1   What is a reference?

In short, references are an acknowledgement of other people's work. They are a way of indicating, according to accepted convention, that you have drawn upon, been inspired by, wish to argue against, someone else; not just anyone, but a particular person, group of people or institution. References name that person or group. References indicate that you are familiar with a 'body of work'. They demonstrate that you have taken the trouble to see who has said what in your field before you.

There are a number of terms that are used to describe different aspects of referencing, and they are not always used consistently. However, it may help to review the following terms: 'reference', 'citation', 'source' and 'bibliography'.

'Reference' is often used as a generic term. Broadly speaking, this is when you identify or 'refer to' someone else, or, more particularly, their work. Your list of references at the end of an essay will contain a series of 'citations'. Citations are more specifically the notes on where to find the material you have cited: Redman, P. and Maples, W. (2011) *Good Essay Writing: A Social*

Sciences Guide, 4th edn, London, Sage. However, 'citation' and 'reference' are often used interchangeably. 'Source' is a bit more distinctive. Sources may be individuals you have interviewed, local government archives, a website, or a particular journal or key author. When you are writing your essay, you need to cite your sources, and provide a list of references for them at the end. In some disciplines and in different countries, you may instead be asked for a bibliography at the end of your work. Again, there is a bit of an overlap in the common use of 'reference list' and 'bibliography', but broadly speaking, reference lists are appropriate for shorter, undergraduate essays, where all material that is used to inform the essay will have been directly cited within the text. Bibliographies could well include books and articles, websites, films, etc. that have been employed (for example as 'background' reading) during research but may not have been directly referenced in the final written work. You will more commonly find bibliographies at the end of dissertations, textbooks or monographs.

Reference writing may seem like a banal clerical activity, and it usually takes much longer than you could possibly imagine. So why do you have to do it?

10.2   Why are references needed?

There are several reasons why proper referencing is important. First, as noted above, it acknowledges your sources and demonstrates that you are familiar with the key material on your topic and are knowledgeable about it. Second, it guards against plagiarism, or accusations of plagiarism, since good referencing clearly shows the source of any data or arguments you use that are not your own. Third, good referencing allows the person who is reading your assignment to follow up any work you mention that sounds particularly interesting, or that he or she does not know. In order to do this the reader needs as much information as possible so he or she can more easily find the work in a library, bookshop or on the internet. Fourth, having a sound referencing system will help you remember particular points, or pieces of work and who said or wrote them. Finally, an essay that is properly referenced looks like a professional piece of writing, worthy of academic respect. Put another way:

- References assert the 'authority' of your argument.
- They allow readers to check the accuracy of the claims that your essay makes.
- References allow your readers to look up a source or argument that they want to know more about.
- References act as a reminder to the author of sources used, and make it easier for you to follow up or go back to ideas at a later stage.

- They are part of academic convention; presenting proper references shows you understand academic principles.

Related to this final point, references are also common courtesy. As you are part of an academic community, it is only right and courteous that you should acknowledge the work of others in your community.

10.3   What should be referenced?

The following items need to be referenced:

- Quotations.
- Diagrams, statistical information or maps reproduced or cited in your essay.
- Work that is referred to but not quoted directly (for example, if you have written 'Hall (2004) argues that . . .' or 'Research by Szerszynski (2010) suggests that . . .').
- Otherwise unsubstantiated arguments and assertions (for example, if you have written, 'Several commentators have argued . . .' or 'It is arguable that conventional notions of "normality" have been fundamentally challenged by the disability rights movement', you could then insert a reference or references that indicate to the reader that this idea has a considerable degree of academic respectability – in other words, there are a number of legitimate sources who have made the same or similar suggestions).

10.4   Basic principles

There are many ways to write references, but all have one feature in common: clear, unambiguous information that allows you or your reader to locate the work. Some authors and some academic journals use a footnote numbering system for the abbreviated reference, with the full reference at the bottom of the page or at the end of the text. You may find online support, such as EasyBib (www.easybib.com/ebook/home) or North Carolina State University's Citation Builder (www.lib.ncsu.edu/lobo2/citationbuilder/index.php), helpful in automating your referencing, but please remember that there are different citation styles – for instance, Citation Builder doesn't use the Harvard style (though the Chicago reference list or APA name/date styles are similar) – and that you need to be consistent in your style of referencing. This chapter demonstrates a version of the 'Harvard' author/date system for texts, commonly used in the social sciences. It is perhaps the easiest system available, and you will find it adequate for almost all purposes.

Abbreviated references in the body of the text, including example of single author book

Let's consider the basic principles for abbreviated references appearing in the main body of your essay as used for a book with a single author. Having written a quotation you simply add immediately after it an abbreviated reference, for example:

'The word "race" has been, and still is, associated with ideas of inferiority, superiority, hierarchy and persecution' (Clarke, 2003, p. 38).

Note that the full stop goes outside the bracket since the abbreviated reference is all part of the sentence. If you use the author's name in your sentence, you can also write your reference like this:

Clarke (2003, p. 38) argues that, as a term, 'race' is 'associated with ideas of inferiority, superiority, hierarchy and persecution'.

Abbreviated references should contain information in the following order:

- Author's last name;
- date of publication (make sure this is the date of the edition in your hand or on your screen);
- if applicable (for example if using a direct quotation or referring to a specific point), the page number(s).

If your quote is a long one (more than 30 words or two lines), then it should be indented and you should dispose of opening and closing quotation marks. Your abbreviated reference should then fall in the line immediately following the quotation.

Old age is surrounded with perceptions which have been called the myths of old age (Sidell, 1995). Such myths include that older people are a homogenous group; that ill health can be expected in old age (Sidell, 1995, p. xvi); in turn leading to a commonly held belief that older people are a burden, as they experience such ill health and physical decline. The homogenous grouping of older people together has been robustly challenged (Dressel et al., 1997), with differences along class, gender and race divisions now widely accepted to have an impact on an individual's experience of ageing.

(Innis, 2010, pp. 19–20)

All your abbreviated references must be expanded into full references in a list at the end of your essay.

List of full references at the end of the text

At the end of your essay, in a list headed 'References' or 'Reference List', you need to write out all your references in full, organized alphabetically by authors' surnames. Let's consider first the Clarke example above. In the reference list the entry would be:

Clarke, S. (2003) *Social Theory, Psychoanalysis and Racism*, Houndmills, Palgrave Macmillan.

This entry is typical of those for a book with a single author. All similar entries in the Harvard system should:

- begin with the author's surname and initial(s);
- give the date of publication (of the *relevant* edition);
- give the title of the work;
- give the place of publication and
- name the publisher.

Here is a simple template:

Author's last name, First name initial(s). (date) *Title of the book*, **Location of the publisher, Publisher.**

For books, you won't need to include individual page numbers in the long reference because you've given these to the reader already – however, see below for conventions for journal articles and chapters in books. Your list of references will look similar to the one at the end of this book.

Basic conventions

The example we have just looked at is of a single author book, but of course you will find that material quoted or referred to can come from many different types of sources, and your reference list must reflect this. Unfortunately the basic referencing system needs a little more embellishment to cover the extra details for all but the most straightforward references. More examples of sources commonly used are given below.

First, though, let's just note a few more basic conventions that it is helpful to remember:

- titles of major works, programmes, etc. (such as book and journal titles) are set in *italics* or underlined;
- parts of works or minor works (such as articles within journals or chapters within edited collections) are put in 'single quotation marks'.

Sometimes you will need to reference a number of works by the same author that happen to have been published in the same year. How do you differentiate them when giving an abbreviated reference? The solution is to label them '2010a', '2010b' and so on. Thus, you might write, 'Szerszynski (2010a, 2010b) argues that . . .'. When giving the full references at the end of the essay, you would then list them with the 2010a entry followed by the 2010b entry. (The order of 'a' and 'b' is usually determined by the order in which they occur in the essay.)

If in your essay you have more than one text to reference in one citation, list them alphabetically, for example: (Clarke, 2003; Frosh et al., 2002; Haywood and Mac an Ghaill, 2003).

eBooks

The protocol for eBook references is much the same as for printed volumes. However, some eBook readers don't list page numbers. If this is the case, and you wish to use a direct quote or specific argument, you will need to include the chapter in which the quote or argument appears in your in-text citation. In addition, your full reference should indicate that your source is an eBook.

Online sources

Where you have found a source online, you need to indicate this. The convention is similar to that listed above, but you will also need to include the exact URL and the date that you accessed the source.

Immediately below you will find examples of common academic sources, with common reference examples for printed and online forms. We have also included examples of sources that arc only available online, such as online conferences or YouTube clips.

Books

Abbreviated (in-text) reference:
Single author:

(Marx, 2004/1888, p. 15)

Note that the recent edition date is listed first and the date of the edition from which it was derived is listed second, separated by '/'.

Matthews notes that 'kittens are often delightful' (2010, ch. 6)

In this example, the eBook reader did not access page numbers, so the location of the direct quote is indicated as best as possible, by chapter.

Where there are two authors, an example of the form for the abbreviated reference would be:

(Haywood and Mac an Ghaill, 2003).

Where there are more than two authors, the abbreviated reference gives the first author's surname then 'et al.' (meaning 'and others'):

(Frosh et al., 2002, p. 18)

Full reference, print, eBook, and online:
The full reference lists all the authors, in the order in which they appear in the work itself, which might not be alphabetically.

Print:

Haywood, C. and Mac an Ghaill, M. (2003) *Men and Masculinities: Theory, Research and Social Practice*, Buckingham, Open University Press.
Frosh, S., Phoenix, A. and Pattman, P. (2002) *Young Masculinities: Understanding Boys in Contemporary Society*, London, Palgrave.

eBook (e.g. Kindle):

Marx, K. and Engels, F. (2004/1888) *The Communist Manifesto* (ebook), New York, Bantam.

Online:

Willie, S.S. (2003) *Acting Black: College, Identity and the Performance of Race* (online), http://library.open.ac.uk/linking/index.php?id=311027 (Accessed 10 April 2010).

Edited collection

This refers to a collection of chapters, articles or extracts compiled by one or more editors.

Abbreviated reference:

(Steinberg and Johnson, 2004)

However, it is unusual to quote directly from the editors of a book (unless from their introduction). It is more common to cite a chapter *within* the book, in which case you should follow the instructions below.

Full reference:

If you simply refer to the book itself, treat the name(s) of the editor(s) as the author(s). The abbreviated reference: (Steinberg and Johnson, 2004), for example, would have this reference list entry:

> Steinberg, D.L. and Johnson, R. (eds) (2004) *Blairism and the War of Persuasion: Labour's Passive Revolution*, London, Lawrence and Wishart.

Chapter, article or extract in an edited collection

If you are quoting from one of the articles/extracts in the collection, the abbreviated reference should give the name(s) of the author(s) of that article/extract and the date of the edited collection. For example, as well as being the editors of the above collection, Steinberg and Johnson also wrote several of its chapters (although, in both cases, with Johnson as the first named author).

Abbreviated reference:

> (Johnson and Steinberg, 2004)

Full reference:

> Johnson, R. and Steinberg, D.L. (2004) 'Distinctiveness and difference with New Labour', in Steinberg, D.L. and Johnson, R. (eds), *Blairism and the War of Persuasion: Labour's Passive Revolution*, London, Lawrence and Wishart.

Some formats require that, in a full reference, you state the page numbers of articles/extracts in edited collections in the same manner as articles in journals (see below). However, this practice is not uniform.

Journal/periodical article

Abbreviated reference:

> (Torfason and Ingram, 2010)

or, if you are quoting directly, or summarizing a specific argument:

> (Torfason and Ingram, 2010, p. 366)

More than two authors follows the same format as the book example, above:

(Willis et al., 2010, p. 250)

Full reference:

For the full article within a journal reference you include details of the journal volume/issue number and the page numbers between which the article appears, but you don't include place of publication or publisher's name. For example:

Torfason, M.T. and Ingram, P. (2010) 'The global rise of democracy: A network account', *American Sociological Review*, vol. 75, no. 3, pp. 355–77.

Online:

Articles from online journals require some additional information. Sometimes it is enough to give the URL for the article, but, depending on what sort of access you have to the journal (which will depend on such things as your university library's permissions, or whether the journal is an 'open commons' journal) the direct URL may not work for others. If you know there is restricted access, it may be best to give the 'home page' URL for the journal, and then list the DOI (which is the unique code for the article itself).

Torfason, M.T. and Ingram, P. (2010) 'The global rise of democracy: A network account', *American Sociological Review*, vol. 75, no. 3 (online), pp. 355–77, http://asr.sagepub.com/content/75/3/355.full, doi: 10.1177/0003122410372230 (Accessed 13 August 2010).

Newspaper article

These follow much the same pattern as journal articles, although omitting in the full reference the page numbers between which the item appears.

Abbreviated reference:

(Stratton, 2010, p. 13)

Full reference:

Stratton, Allegra (2010) 'PM: we're junior partners with US', *Guardian*, 17 May, p. 13.

Notice that the full reference includes the specific date of publication after the newspaper's title.

Online full reference:

Brown, Mark (2010) 'Linguist on mission to save Inuit "fossil language" disappearing with the ice', *Guardian*, 13 August (online) http://www.guardian.co.uk/world/2010/aug/13/inuit-language-culture-threatened (Accessed 13 August 2010).

Film, television or DVD material

If you are doing a media studies or film degree, your course may have particular conventions for citing films, television or radio programmes and series. On many film courses, the director takes the place of the 'author'. However, if you are researching screenplays, you may find the convention of the screenwriter taking the 'author' place. You will notice that the standard format presented below deviates from the Harvard 'author/date' template, with the title of the film coming first.

Abbreviated reference:

(*Little Miss Sunshine*, 2006)
(*Curb Your Enthusiasm*, 2009)

Full reference:
For a film:

Title of Film (year of distribution) medium (i.e. film or DVD), directed by Director Name, Place of distribution, Distribution company.

Example:

Little Miss Sunshine (2006) film, directed by Jonathan Dayton and Valerie Faris, Burbank, Fox Searchlight.

For a television programme (or series):

Title of the series or programme (year of transmission), type of broadcast, 'Title of episode' (Series, episode number) directed by Director name, Distributor.

Example:

Xena Warrior Princess (1998), television series, 'Endgame' (Series 4, episode 20) directed by Garth Maxwell, Renaissance Pictures.

However, you may not be able to get all of this information for some television programmes. 'Ephemeral' programmes, like the news or talk shows, may be referenced like this:

Title of the Series or Programme, type of broadcast, Channel, Date of broadcast.

The Daily Show with Jon Stewart, comedy/news television programme, More 4, 13 August 2010 (originally broadcast 12 August 2010).

In this case, the programme is a topical daily programme initially broadcast in the US; the version that is cited here is a 'repeat' transmission, broadcast a day later.

For a film, TV or radio programme accessed online:

The Human Footprint (2010) television documentary, Channel 4 On Demand (online)   http://www.channel4.com/programmes/the-human-footprint/4od (Accessed 13 August 2010).

Forums

In general, you will want to cite a particular message to a forum and should, therefore, identify the author. Before doing so, however, you must check that the author is happy for you to quote them. Notice that if there is a series of postings by the same author you should include the time of the posting, as well as the date.

Abbreviated reference:

(Bhote, 2010)

Full reference:

Last Name, Initials. (year) 'Subject of message', message to Name of the Forum, date and time.
Bhote, K. (2010) 'Twitter as a research tool', message to H800 Technology-enhanced learning: practices and debates, Tutor-group forum, 23 June 07:02.

Blogs

Harvard referencing for blogs is not dissimilar to that for online journals and follows the author/date format. One difference may be if the blogger uses an alias – in which case, the alias should be used instead of the author's name.

Abbreviated reference:

(Weller, 2010)

Full reference:
The full reference follows this format: Author, A. (year of publication/last updated) 'Title of message', *Title of Website*, blog entry posted day/month of posted message (online), URL (date accessed).

Weller, M. (2010) 'For the last time – open access is not like stealing bread', *The Ed Techie*, blog entry, 30 July, http://nogoodreason.typepad.co.uk/no_ good_reason/2010/07/for-the-last-time-open-access-is-not-like-stealing- bread.html (Accessed 13 August 2010).

Podcasts and iTunes

The Harvard system for referencing podcasts is not dissimilar to that for film or TV programmes. Example:

Abbreviated reference:

(*Thinking Allowed*, 2010)

Full reference:
The full reference format is as follows: *Title of podcast* (year of publication), podcast type, podcaster, place of podcast, URL (date accessed).

Examples:

Thinking Allowed (2010) podcast radio programme, BBC Radio 4, UK, http://www.bbc.co.uk/podcasts/series/ta (Accessed 12 August 2010).
Does Prison Work? (2010) iTunes video, The Open University, Milton Keynes (Accessed 13 August 2010).

YouTube

YouTube clips are incredibly varied, but broadly follow the film referencing format in the Harvard system.

Abbreviated reference:

(*Bert on how the internet has changed his life*, 2010)

Full reference:

The full reference format looks like this: *Title of Item* (year of distribution), YouTube video, added by name of who uploaded it, URL (date accessed).

Example:

Bert on how the internet has changed his life (2010) YouTube video, added by raceonline2012, http://www.youtube.com/watch?v=xVDBeK7U4PI&feature=channel (Accessed 13 August 2010).

10.5 Advanced referencing

In the preceding section we explored some of the referencing conventions that you are likely to use fairly frequently. In what follows, we will investigate less common and more complex referencing issues, including further examples of electronic sources.

Printed sources

An author quoted in another text

Sometimes you will come across a quotation or reference in a book you are reading and decide to reference it in your own work. In such circumstances it is good practice to find the original source to check that the details are correct (for example, has the original author been misquoted or her argument distorted?). However, particularly if the source is obscure, untranslated or long out of print, this may not be possible. For example, in her book *Feminism, Theory and the Politics of Difference* (1999), Chris Weedon quotes from a book by Emma Drake, published in 1901, to illustrate the point that women's reproductive capacity has frequently been seen to define their gender. If we were to use this quotation ourselves, it is possible we would not be able to find the original source, so we make an accommodation.

Abbreviated reference:

(Drake, quoted in Weedon, 1999, p. 7)

Full reference:

Weedon, C. (1999) *Feminism, Theory and the Politics of Difference*, Oxford, Blackwell.

Government/official publication

Abbreviated reference:

(Department of Social Security, 1999)

Full reference:

> Department of Social Security (1999) 'Action across the UK', *Opportunity for All: Tackling Poverty and Social Exclusion,* London, The Stationery Office (September, Cm 4445).

Online reference:

> House of Commons (2003) *Hansard*, 2 July, Column 407 (online), http://www.parliament.the-stationery-office.co.uk/pa/cm200203/cmhansrd/vo030702/debtext/30702-10.htm (Accessed 13 February 2009).
>
> MacDonald, Z., Tinsley, L., Collingwood, J., Jamieson, P. and Pudney, S. (2005) 'Measuring the harm from illegal drugs using the Drug Harm Index', Home Office Online Report, 24 May, http://www.homeoffice.gov.uk/rds/pdfs05/rdsolr2405.pdf (Accessed 28 May 2005).

Non-governmental organization publication

Abbreviated reference:

> (British Psychological Society, 2003)

Full reference:

> British Psychological Society (2003) 'Child protection – protecting children and young people from abuse, harm and neglect: the responsibilities of chartered psychologists', Leicester, British Psychological Society.

Online reference:

> Greenpeace (2010) 'Briefing – opportunities and challenges for off-shore wind power in Britain', London, Greenpeace, http://www.greenpeace.org.uk/files/pdfs/climate/Outline_briefing_offshore_wind_20100114.pdf (Accessed 13 August 2010).

Specialist learning guides or audio-visual material

This refers to the support material that may come with your module or on your course. Material of this kind may not have an identifiable 'author'. For example, for an Open University DVD, audio programme or assignment handbook, the 'author' should be identified as the university itself.

Abbreviated reference:

> (The Open University, 2005)

Full reference, for a DVD, for instance:

The Open University (2005) DVD2, Theme Lecture 1, 'Powers and structures', DD203 *Power, Dissent, Equality: Understanding Contemporary Politics*, Milton Keynes, The Open University.

Other electronic sources

Online book

As noted above, eBooks or books accessed through an online library will have place of publication and publisher details and should be referenced as normal – with the URL and date of access noted at the end of the reference. Some books that are accessible online are out of print, in which case you will be unable to cite the location and name of the publisher. In this case you should list the book by author, as usual, and cite the URL and access date in place of location and name of publisher. Open source publications will often be published by a university or the university's in-house publisher, in which case, this should be listed, along with the URL and date of access.

For example:

Mill, J.S. (1859) *On Liberty*, http://www.bartleby.com/130/index.html (Accessed 13 June 2005).

and

Resch, R.P. (1992) *Althusser and the Renewal of Marxist Social Theory*, Berkeley, University of California Press, http://ark.cdlib.org/ark:/13030/ft3n39n8x3/ (Accessed 19 May 2005).

Online research project:

Dunne, M., Humphreys, S. and Leach, F. (2003) 'Gender violence in school', School of Education, University of Sussex, http://portal. unesco.org/education/en/file_download.php/ee2258a3769cd087cc2 453acdbe3910G-enderandviolenceinschools.doc (Accessed 19 May 2005).

Online conference paper

Hosu, A. (2003) 'Identity politics and narrativity', paper presented to The Second Tampere Conference on Narrative, Tampere, 26–8 June, http://www.uta.fi/conference/narrative/papers/hosu.pdf (Accessed 19 May 2005).

CD-ROM

Craig, E. (ed.) (1998) *Encyclopedia of Philosophy* (CD-ROM), London, Routledge.

Personal communication

If you quote something said in a conversation or letter, you should note this.

Abbreviated reference:

(Mooney, 2010, personal communication with author)

You may not need to include this in the references list, but if you need to (for example, if you have quoted directly or used any substantial points from your source), then you should add the initials to the list of references and the date of the correspondence or conversation:

Full reference:

Mooney, G. (2010) email communication, 18 May.

Identifying the details for references

Publication details are given near the front of the book on the 'imprint' page, which usually comes after the title page. Please check carefully the particular notes for each component (date, edition, place, publisher).

Different publication dates

The date of publication you need is the latest year noted in the book that you have. For instance, *The German Ideology*, a key text in classical Marxist theory, first appeared in the nineteenth century. However, one edition of this text was published in 1974. If you are making a point that draws generally on this work, the reference will read:

Marx, K. and Engels, F. (1974) *The German Ideology*, London, Lawrence and Wishart.

Where dates for reprints are noted, use the year given against the copyright (©) line.

Retaining early publication dates

For specific points, including quotations from an early work, where you want to include the early date but your reading is from a modern reproduction, note the more recent date first, separated from the original date by a forward slash.

Abbreviated reference

(Marx, 1974/1846, p. 26)

The page number refers, of course, to the modern edition.

Full reference:

Marx, K. and Engels, F. (1974/1846) *The German Ideology*, London, Lawrence and Wishart.

Edition numbers

Books are not only reprinted but can be revised and republished as a new *edition*. This often occurs when new material is added because the book has become dated. In fact, the 1974 copy of *The German Ideology* cited above is the second edition of this particular version of the book. A first edition was published in 1970. Because second and subsequent editions contain alterations, it is important to tell the reader which version you're working from. The full reference should therefore read:

Marx, K. and Engels, F. (1974/1846) *The German Ideology*, 2nd edn, London, Lawrence and Wishart.

Publisher and place of publication

Assuming that you are writing in Britain or for a British audience, you need to quote the British place of publication of British publishers. For example, Sage is based in London, so you put London as the place of publication. If you are writing in the US, for a US audience, you should give the US address of the publisher if there is one. Sage, for example, also has a base in Thousand Oaks, California – so, Thousand Oaks is the place of publication. Be sure to give the place of publication (that is, the city or town where the publisher is based) and not the place where the book was printed.

Collaborative publishing

Sometimes books are brought out by more than one publisher. Some university course books are collaborations of this kind. In such cases, name both publishers. The place of publication will be indicated on the imprint page.

Abbreviated reference:

(Andrews and Saward, 2005)

Full reference:

Andrews, G. and Saward, M. (eds) (2005) *Living Political Ideas*, Edinburgh/ Milton Keynes, Edinburgh University Press/The Open University.

10.6   Compiling your references

It's a good idea to familiarize yourself with the basic principles for writing references before you begin to access your sources. Then, *at the time* you are researching your sources, keep to hand this chapter. Note down all the details you will require including page numbers for journal and newspaper articles, and the exact page number for any quotes or key ideas you think you might use. It is also good practice to note down where you found your material: Google Scholar, the local library, borrowed from a friend, etc., in case you need to find it again. Almost all of us have at some time omitted to note our references properly and learned how difficult it is to trace the reference details afterwards – usually at the very moment that the essay is due to hand in.

There are a number of software packages, such as EndNote or RefWorks, that make this process much easier, compiling the reference information into alphabetized and searchable data sets. Your university might have its own referencing package as part of its student support or library facilities. You would be well advised to make use of such a facility from the beginning of your studies.

In terms of producing your references for an essay, perhaps the best advice is to try to remember the basic referencing format and then look up the further guidance details from this book as you need them. Certainly you should not be intimidated by what looks like a complex process. Get started on the basics, using the guidance above, and then check the specific examples as the need arises.

Summary

- Referencing is a basic academic skill and it is almost certain that you will be expected to use references accurately on undergraduate courses.
- To write a reference using the Harvard system you should give an abbreviated reference in the text and full details in a list of references at the end of the text.
- Abbreviated references in the text are written: (Author's last name, publication date). If you are using a direct quote or specific point, you will also need to include the page number: (Author's last name, publication date, page number).
- Full references at the end of the text are listed alphabetically by author/ originator.
- References for different publications by the same author in the same year are distinguished using 'a', 'b', etc. according to order in which they appear in the essay.
- Full references at the end of the text for a single author book are written: Author's surname and Initials, publication date, *Title* (italicized or underlined), Place of publication, Publisher. Electronic references follow similar principles as those for printed texts but must also include the URL and date of access.
- References to chapters in edited collections, to journal and newspaper articles, and to various other sources are given in slightly different ways. Titles of chapters, journal and newspaper articles are given in quotes: 'Distinctiveness and difference with New Labour'.
- Note down your reference details at the time you are finding your material.
- Appendix A includes some abbreviations that are sometimes used when referencing, particularly when using the alternative footnote numbering system.

Self-test

1 Why is referencing important?
2 What style of referencing should you adopt for your essays? (Answer: whichever system is recommended on your course or by your tutor.)
3 What resources might you use to help you with getting your referencing in the right format?
4 Using the Harvard system, what is the basic format for: an abbreviated (in-text) reference and a full (reference list) reference?

11

Some Common Worries

- Writing too much or too little
- Using the 'I' word, subjectivity and objectivity
- Using your own experience
- Presentation, spelling, grammar and punctuation
- Plagiarism and poor academic practice

It is difficult to identify or predict all the worries that you may have in writing essays. But there are a few important points to know about and some things to avoid, so read this chapter carefully.

11.1 Writing too much or too little

Most essays have word limits. Many students point out that they could easily write a whole lot more on any one topic. Indeed, people write 80,000-word books on the sort of issues that you address in your essays, so everyone knows that word limits can be rather restrictive. However, they are not set merely to irritate you. Shorter essays are an important academic tool. In writing them, you learn how to prioritize and select material, and how to condense big topics into a punchy, easily digested form. These are academic skills that you will need even in writing much longer pieces. Painful though it may be, if you're writing too much, be ruthless. Concentrate on the biggest, most important arguments and examples – and cut the rest. Your work will almost certainly be better for it.

Remember that on many courses you will need to provide a word count at the end of your essay and that marks may be deducted if you have exceeded this (always check the regulations covering the specific course that you are studying). Furthermore, some markers may feel that writing over length allows you to cover a topic in more detail than other people and thus confers an unfair advantage on you.

If, on the other hand, you find it difficult to fill the page, it is essential to ask yourself whether you are addressing the question adequately; whether there is enough depth or breadth to your answer, or whether you have provided appropriate support for your argument in the form of examples or illustrations. Reread the assignment question (and any guidance notes) for clues as to what might be 'missing'.

11.2   Using the 'I' word, 'subjectivity' and 'objectivity'

Perhaps the best way to find out whether the use of 'I' is appropriate to the particular course you are studying is to check with the person marking your work. Sometimes you will be told that the first-person pronoun ('I') should be avoided (for example, that you should not write 'In this essay I intend to explore . . .'). In this case, you can often ignore personal pronouns completely (for example, by writing 'This essay will explore . . .'). In fact, there are no hard and fast rules about using 'I' in social science essays, and different disciplines (and different tutors) tend to adopt different conventions.

'I' is sometimes thought to indicate a lack of objectivity, but it is important to separate out the different issues here. It is possible to be objective and use the first-person pronoun. It is possible to be utterly subjective in your writing without using 'I' at all. Phrases such as 'I think', 'I believe' and 'I feel', however, risk you making assertions without offering evidence or developing a logical argument – and this is the real concern for social science writing. Some social scientists argue that it is better to be upfront about our subject positions or investments in a topic. For instance, the introduction to *Good Essay Writing* might have mentioned that our 'investment' in writing this book is because we've seen students enjoy being able to better and more easily express themselves after they've been given a few clear pointers on essay writing. This doesn't make the book or its suggestions less valid, but it does help you understand why we've written it.

You may also be asked for some self-reflection on your experience of doing the assignment: in this case, it is generally accepted that you will reflect using the first-person pronoun. Even in this case, however, you will want to avoid the excessive repetition of 'I' – as with any other word or phrase.

11.3   Using your own experience

Some essay questions will explicitly ask you to draw on your own personal experience – indeed, autobiography is a recognized research method in the social sciences. Additionally, relevant personal experience is sometimes used to add 'colour' to an argument or to grab the reader's attention.

Having said this, there can be a danger that, in the context of social scientific writing, personal experience will sound like bar-room philosophy. In other words, it will be little more than unsubstantiated personal opinion. A good rule is, therefore, to avoid the use of personal experience in academic writing unless you are explicitly asked to do otherwise.

11.4   Presentation, spelling, grammar and punctuation

Your essays will be marked first and foremost on their content, however, your work should also be well-presented (see also Section 3.3). Your course or module may have specific presentation conventions, but in general you should ensure that in the header for each page you include:

- your name and/or personal identifier
- the module or course number and the assignment number/name
- the name of your tutor
- the date of submission.

In addition, you should have a title, either on a title page or at the top of page 1, and each page should be numbered, including the reference list page, but *excluding* the title page if you are asked for this.

Correct spelling, grammar and punctuation are part of a good presentation – and are important in essay writing. The baseline here is that essays should be readable and make sense. Your spelling, grammar and punctuation need to be good enough to communicate effectively to your reader and, at degree level or equivalent, this implies the ability to use conventions of spelling, grammar and punctuation accurately.

As a result, you should choose your words carefully in order to say what you mean – and mean what you say. Use of 'jargon' words has already been mentioned in 'Clear sentences and paragraphs' (in Section 8.4). If you use abbreviations or foreign words, make sure you use them correctly (Appendix A has a list of those commonly found). To help you with standard English words, you should have a dictionary (Chambers, Oxford or Webster's are all good) to hand (don't rely on spell check), and you may also find it helpful to have a style guide, such as *The Oxford A–Z of Grammar and Punctuation*

(Seely, 2009) to help with solving a variety of writing dilemmas, such as when to use a colon or semi-colon, or whether the full stop (period) should go inside or outside the close brackets (parentheses). For a more light-hearted and rather zealous approach to grammar and punctuation, you might also find Lynne Truss's *Eats, Shoots and Leaves: The Zero Tolerance Approach to Punctuation* both helpful and enjoyable.

It is good practice to read aloud, to yourself or a trusted peer, the whole of your essay. If you stumble in reading, this may be an indication that a sentence is not as clear as it might be. You may also ask someone else to read your work before you submit it: often a fresh set of eyes will catch errors that you have missed. This is generally considered to be good practice and is why professional writers have editors. One further point – a trusted peer is *not* someone who will tell you everything you've written is marvellous. Ideally, you should ask someone who is willing to be politely critical of your work, remembering that they are commenting on the essay, not on you personally.

11.5 Plagiarism and poor academic practice

The whole of this guide is premised on supporting good academic practice and helping you to avoid poor academic practice. Poor academic practice includes things like not answering the question, failing to follow your tutor's guidance, writing incoherent sentences or over-using colloquial phrases, insufficient research, superficial reading, etc. However, possibly the greatest bugbear for teachers in higher education is the poor academic practice of plagiarism.

Plagiarism means using someone else's work and passing it off as your own. It refers to copying other people's work word for word, or making only minor changes to it with the intention of representing their words as yours. This does not mean that you are forbidden to use any word or phrase that appears in a text from which you are working. In particular, you will almost certainly need to repeat technical vocabulary. For example, it would look rather odd if an essay on Marxist theory avoided key conceptual categories such as 'class struggle' or 'relation to the means of production'. The problem occurs when you recycle whole sentences or paragraphs without indicating that these are quotations, or paraphrased from your original source.

Sometimes plagiarism is clear cut and easily recognizable – but sometimes it is the result of other poor academic practices. Of course, it is easy enough to avoid intentionally passing off someone else's work as your own. However, some students seem to copy or closely paraphrase other people's work without realizing. How can the risk of this be minimized?

There are, perhaps, three main reasons why students sometimes plagiarize inadvertently:

- bad note-taking, including poor referencing;
- lack of confidence;
- failure to understand what it means to 'write in your own words'.

The first two are fairly easy to address. Bad note-taking can lead to inadvertent plagiarism when, in preparing for an essay, students copy material into their notes without using quotation marks or references. This material then risks being transferred directly into the final essay which, in consequence, will be partially, if inadvertently, plagiarized. This can be exacerbated when using sources that allow you to cut and paste, and even more so sources like Wikipedia which may themselves be inadequately referenced (see Section 5.3). The solution, of course, is always to use quotation marks and to record references when making notes (see Section 5.2).

Lack of confidence can result in inadvertent plagiarism when students stick very closely to the original wording of a source because they are unsure of its exact meaning. In such circumstances, students may feel that copying or close paraphrasing reduces the risk of 'getting it wrong'. The problem is that the marker won't be able to tell how much the students have understood and, in consequence, won't be able to award them many, if any, marks. The solution in this case is to take time to ensure that you fully understand what you are writing about and, when necessary, to ask for help from your tutor and/or fellow students. Although it may seem pedestrian, you should also try to express ideas *as you understand them*. Particularly at the earlier stages of your studies, it may be more pedagogically productive not to use all of the academic vocabulary introduced on your course – at least until you feel more confident of its meaning.

Failure to understand what it means to 'write in your own words' is perhaps more complicated and requires a more detailed response.

What does it mean to 'write in your own words'?

In order to answer this question we need to look at some worked examples. These, and the commentary that accompanies them, are drawn from the Open University study support material, 'Writing in your own words' (Redman, 2002).

Imagine that you need to use the following invented conversation between two students for an essay on issues in teaching and learning social science. You need to distil their different positions, and to represent them accurately, but in your own words.

Becky: 'I don't know why I decided to do this course. It is all jargon and theory and none of it makes any sense.

Elsie: Really? I like all the debates and the jargon is just like learning another language, but one that's useful, not like Latin or C-plus.

Becky: Latin is infinitely more useful than, I don't know, Baudrillard. The Gulf War never happened? What does that mean? And anyway, it happened twice.

Elsie: I think Baudrillard meant that on the one hand the war wasn't a war in the sense that two powers were fighting over territory or a political ideal, but that we just treated it like a war because there were armies involved and bombs and destruction. For most people the 'experience' of the war was only representation – what they saw of the fighting on TV. There's also the thing of euphemisms, so there's 'collateral damage', which actually means that a village has been bombed and civilians have died.

Becky: More jargon!

Elsie: Well, sort of. I mean what Baudrillard is saying is that it is all euphemism and representation, that all we can ever know is what we understand through signs and representation. The example of the Gulf War is used to explore how things have reached a kind of peak of 'hyper-reality', divorced from the real, visceral nature of war.

Becky: I can sort of see that. Like how during the Vietnam War the government suddenly realized that showing American soldiers coming back in body bags wasn't winning sympathy from the rest of America for the action in Vietnam, instead it was turning people against the idea of war altogether.

Elsie: I think I see what you're saying –

Becky: So, the point is that the government then tried to clean up the image of the war – and not let the news programmes show the coffins being unloaded from the planes, but the damage was already done: public opinion had already shifted. So you're saying that Baudrillard is pointing out that the news is so sanitized now that it is hard to imagine what's really going on. That it is just a simulacrum?

Elsie: I thought you hated 'jargon' . . .

(Word count: 364)

Below you will find two versions of this dialogue, rewritten for inclusion in an essay.

Version A

A discussion between two students, Elsie and Becky, focused on the issue of social science 'jargon'. Becky, in particular, found the ideas of theorists such as Baudrillard obfuscating rather than illuminating. Elsie, however, was able to give a mainly accurate gloss of the main issues and some of the key terms in Baudrillard's article 'The Gulf War did not take place' (1991) and his assertion that symbols have become more real than reality – which he terms 'hyper-reality'. Although Becky misunderstood Elsie's description somewhat, suggesting Baudrillard was concerned with governments' attempts at fabrication, she found herself using Baudrillard's concept of the 'simulacrum' to clarify her point, perhaps undermining her claim that she was unhappy with the 'jargon' on her course.

(Word count: 119)

What does this tell us about 'writing in your own words'? You can see that the paragraph summarizes the main points of Elsie and Becky's discussion, but in the context of the set essay. The summary broadly follows the order of the discussion – though often you will find that it is necessary to shift around the key points. Having said this, it is also clear that, while the paragraph remains true to the original discussion, the vocabulary is substantially different and some less relevant points and details have been omitted. In addition, a note about the source Elsie has drawn upon has been made (Baudrillard's article, 'The Gulf War did not take place'). This is important because students sometimes think that 'writing in your own words' simply means taking a paragraph from a source and changing an odd word, omitting a couple of phrases or rearranging a number of sentences.

For instance, instead of Version A, above, another student might have come up with the following, rather problematic, summary:

Version B

Students Becky and Elsie discussed their social science course, Baudrillard and the problems with jargon. Becky said 'it's all jargon and theory and none of it makes sense'. Elsie pointed out that Baudrillard's ideas about the Gulf War are actually helpful: 'what Baudrillard is saying is that it is all euphemism and representation, that all we can ever know is what we understand through signs and representation. The example of the Gulf War is used to explore how things have reached a kind of peak of "hyper-reality", divorced from the real, visceral nature of war.' Becky didn't quite understand the point that Elsie made, but gave an interesting example of the way the US government tried to control the news of the Vietnam War. In the end, though, she used the term 'simulacrum', suggesting she was starting to feel happier about the use of 'jargon' in her course.

(Word count: 148)

If you compare Version B to the original extract you will see that, although it is not always copied word for word, it follows the original very closely, keeping the same order of the argument, using much of the same vocabulary and so on. In addition, it uses two direct quotes that take up a significant number of words: more problematically, neither helps the reader see whether the author understands the material. While this example wouldn't be seen as plagiarism, it is certainly poor academic practice and would not be awarded many marks, despite accurately recounting some parts of the dialogue.

As we saw in Version A, writing in your own words is very different from this. Rather than copying, it involves reflecting on and digesting someone else's ideas, then producing your own interpretation of these and/or reworking them so that they address the specific task in hand (for example, answering a specific essay question).

Why is avoiding plagiarism so important?

It is important to get on top of this issue for a number of reasons. Most obviously, plagiarized work is likely to attract a fail grade. However, plagiarizing work is also of little educational benefit to you. The process of putting arguments into your own words is a crucial part of grasping ideas and committing them to memory. It also helps you to learn how to use and apply the ideas for *yourself*. Plagiarizing, if nothing else, is a waste of your time since it probably means that you have not thoroughly understood what you have written.

Occasionally some people will deliberately plagiarize in an essay. This is a serious offence, since it is a form of academic theft. In the case of assessed coursework, it is also an attempt to gain qualifications by cheating. Many universities now use plagiarism detection software that identifies essays or sections of essays that replicate material found on a range of websites, or compare students' essays with one another. But tutors often note just how easy it is to spot plagiarism or poor academic practice. How? Tell-tale signs are things like a change of 'voice' (style or vocabulary) from one paragraph to the next, a distinctive turn of phrase from a well-known author, changes in typeface or font, or essays or sections of essays that relate to the question set, but don't answer it, or don't answer it using the recommended texts from the course. Tutors may be sympathetic in the first instance to inadvertent plagiarism and may offer support to develop good academic practice; deliberate plagiarism, however, will almost certainly result in a fail mark and may incur further disciplinary penalties, with serious cases sometimes resulting in expulsion from university.

Summary

- Writing to a word limit is an important academic skill: it teaches you to condense complex material into its component parts, to select and communicate core arguments logically and with appropriate evidence or illustrations.
- Using 'I' is not the same as being subjective, but it can lead to poor social science practice. You should ask your tutor if the use of the first-person pronoun is appropriate on your course.
- Personal experience can be a useful source of evidence and some courses require you to use it. However, be careful to relate it to the course and the essay question and to substantiate your claims.
- Essays are expected to be well-presented, readable and to use conventions of spelling, grammar and punctuation correctly.
- Plagiarism is often unintentional and the result of poor academic practice. However, it is your responsibility to take clear notes, putting ideas and arguments into your own words and quotations in quotation marks or indented; reread your essays, looking for sudden changes in style or tone; and seek help if you do not understand particular points to ensure that, when writing, you can reproduce them in your own words.
- Plagiarism means copying someone else's work and claiming it as your own. Plagiarized essays will normally attract a fail grade. Deliberate plagiarism, which constitutes cheating, may result in disciplinary action.

Self-test

1 How can you ensure you don't write 'too much' or 'too little'?
2 How is using the first-person pronoun different from being subjective, in social science terms?
3 In what sorts of academic writing would you be expected to use 'I'?
4 How can you ensure your grammar, punctuation and spelling are all correct?
5 What is plagiarism and why is it best avoided?
6 What are some of the strategies you can use to avoid plagiarism in your writing?

12

What Tutors Look for When Marking Essays

- Marking schemes: criteria related to grade bands
- Writing skills: 'introductory', 'intermediate' and 'advanced' essays

One of the most frequent and reasonable questions that students ask is: What should I be doing to get a better grade? As you know, the answer to this question will depend on a number of factors. For example, what is required of an essay answer will vary according to the precise question set. Equally, the standard expected of essay writing is likely to be higher on more advanced undergraduate courses than on those at entry level. Similarly, there may be higher expectations towards the end of a module than there were at its start. Having said this, it is possible to specify the various qualities (if only in general terms) that distinguish essays in the different grade bands, and what writing skills may be expected from essays at different levels.

Health warning

This chapter has been included to give you a *broad indication of what may be expected, in general, for different grades.* In the UK, grade bands are often defined in relation to 'learning outcomes' that draw on specified 'subject benchmarks' and 'key skills' (see, for example: www.qaa.ac.uk). Individual courses or modules will have their own specific requirements for each of the grade ranges. These requirements will vary depending on whether a module is at a more or less advanced stage of undergraduate study. As a result, where they are available, you may want to look at the learning outcomes specified for your particular course of study. However, you should remember that grading an essay is always a matter of weighing up not only the structure, content and style of the essay, but the interplay between these, together with the interplay between any number of the different intellectual challenges built into the assignment. For all these reasons you should not expect the grading criteria for a specific module to map exactly on to what is set out here.

12.1   Marking schemes: criteria related to grade bands

In this chapter you will find guidelines adapted from those produced by the British Psychological Society (BPS, 1994) in conjunction with the Association of Heads of Psychology Departments and information from across a range of university institutions world wide. They do not correspond to the specific policy of any specific higher education institution, but they should give you an idea of the sorts of *general* things markers are likely to consider for different grade ranges. Remember, what is expected for a particular module for a particular grade may differ from these guidelines. Remember, too, you won't have to do well in every area to get a particular grade. For example, your depth of insight into theoretical issues may compensate for slightly weaker coverage of the evidence, or your understanding of the material may compensate for weaknesses in the coherence of your argument. It may also be the case that some of these criteria will be more relevant to advanced courses of undergraduate study (see Section 12.2 below).

Many of the terms used below (for example, 'developing an argument') have been explored in greater detail earlier in this guide.

Descriptor	UK university		US university		Other			
Excellent Pass	1st	70+	A	4.0	85+	10	Perfect	High Distinction
			A–	3.7		9	Very good	
Good Pass	2:1	60–69	B	3.0	70–84	8	Good	Distinction
			B+	2.7		7	More than sufficient	
Clear Pass	2:2	50–59	C	2.0	55–69	6	Sufficient	Credit
			C+	1.7				
Bare Pass	3rd	40–49	D	1.0	40–54	5	Nearly sufficient	Pass

(Continued)

(Continued)

Descriptor	UK university		US university		Other			
Bare Fail	Fail	30–39	Fail	0.0	30–39	4	Insufficient	Fail
						3	Strongly insufficient	
Clear Fail	Fail	0–29	Fail		15–29	2	Poor	Fail
Bad Fail					0–14	1	Very poor	

An essay in the top band (excellent pass) will meet or exceed the very highest expectations for undergraduate work and is likely to:

- provide a comprehensive and accurate response to the question, demonstrating a breadth and depth of reading and understanding of relevant arguments and issues;
- show a sophisticated ability to synthesize a wide range of material;
- show a sophisticated ability to outline, analyse and contrast complex competing positions and to evaluate their strengths and weaknesses effectively;
- demonstrate clarity of argument and expression;
- develop a sophisticated argument, demonstrating logical reasoning and the effective use of well-selected examples and evidence;
- where appropriate, demonstrate an ability to apply ideas to new material or in a new context;
- demonstrate depth of insight into theoretical issues;
- demonstrate an ability to write from 'within' a perspective or theory, including the ability to utilize appropriate social scientific concepts and vocabulary;
- show a creative or original approach (within the constraints of academic rigour);
- use a standard referencing system accurately.

A good pass will meet most of the higher expectations of the course or module and is likely to:

- provide a generally accurate and well-informed answer to the question;
- be reasonably comprehensive;
- draw on a range of sources;
- be well organized and structured;
- demonstrate an ability to develop a strong and logical line of argument, supported by appropriate examples and evidence;
- show an ability to synthesize a wide range of material;

- show an ability to outline, analyse and contrast more complex competing positions, and to evaluate their strengths and weaknesses effectively;
- demonstrate the ability to work with theoretical material effectively and some confidence in handling social scientific concepts and vocabulary;
- where appropriate, demonstrate an ability to apply ideas to new material or in a new context;
- show a good understanding of the material;
- be clearly presented;
- use a standard referencing system accurately.

A clear pass will meet all of the basic expectations of the course and is likely to:

- give an adequate answer to the question, though one dependent on commentaries or a limited range of source material;
- be generally accurate, although with some omissions and minor errors;
- develop and communicate a basic logical argument with some use of appropriate supporting examples and evidence;
- demonstrate an ability to synthesize a range of material;
- demonstrate an ability to outline, analyse and contrast competing positions, and to begin to evaluate their strengths and weaknesses (although this may be derivative);
- demonstrate a basic ability to address theoretical material and to use appropriate social scientific concepts and vocabulary;
- be written in the author's own words;
- show an understanding of standard referencing conventions, although containing some errors and/or omissions.

A bare pass will meet some or many of the basic expectations of the course or module and is likely to:

- demonstrate basic skills in the areas identified in the 'clear pass' band;

but may also:

- answer the question tangentially;
- miss one (or more) key points;
- contain a number of inaccuracies or omissions;
- show only sparse coverage of relevant material;
- fail to support arguments with adequate evidence;
- be over-dependent on source material;
- contain only limited references.

A bare fail will not meet many of the basic expectations of the course or module and is likely to:

- fail to answer the question;
- contain limited appropriate material;
- show some evidence of relevant reading but provide only cursory coverage with a number of errors, omissions or irrelevances such that the writer's understanding of fundamental points is in question;
- be disorganized;
- contain much inappropriate material;
- lack any real argument or fail to support an argument with evidence;
- demonstrate a lack of understanding of social scientific concepts and vocabulary
- demonstrate an inability to deploy social scientific writing skills such as skills of critical evaluation, synthesis, and so on;
- be unacceptably dependent on sources;
- be plagiarized (sometimes);
- demonstrate problems in the use of appropriate writing conventions such that the essay's meaning is frequently obscured;
- omit some or many references.

A clear or bad fail will meet few if any of the basic expectations of the course and is likely to:

- show a profound misunderstanding of basic material;
- show a complete failure to understand or answer the question;
- provide totally inadequate information;
- be incoherent;
- be plagiarized (sometimes);
- omit references.

12.2 Writing skills: 'introductory', 'intermediate' and 'advanced' essays

As you move from entry level to more advanced undergraduate courses it is likely that you will be expected to develop and demonstrate an increasing range of essay writing skills (see Sections 3.2 and 4.1). For example, you may be expected to write from 'within' a particular perspective (see Section 8.4), handle more complex theories or systematically interrogate original sources (see Section 5.1).

A general guide of this kind cannot give you a full breakdown of the skills that will be relevant to every course that you may take. What it tries to do is provide an outline of 'core' skills. Individual courses may emphasize different parts of these core skills or may involve specific skills of their own (for example, project writing, employing specific research methods, using graphs to present information). Individual essays may also require you to emphasize some core skills more than others. As a result of these factors, you will need to adapt what is set out below according to the demands of different questions and different courses.

We look now in detail at the various criteria that distinguish 'basic' or success-ful 'introductory' undergraduate essays from 'intermediate' and 'advanced' essays.

The 'introductory' level essay

Introductions are likely to demonstrate:

- a clear understanding of the scope of the question and what is required;
- the ability to 'signpost' the shape of the essay's argument clearly and concisely;
- a basic ability to define key terms.

Main sections are likely to demonstrate some or all of the following, depending on what the question requires:

- an ability to construct a basic argument that engages with the question;
- the ability to précis aspects of relevant material clearly and concisely, often relying on commentaries and other secondary sources;
- the ability to outline, analyze and interpret evidence, arguments and the basics of relevant theories;
- the ability to support arguments with appropriate evidence and examples drawn from different sources;
- an ability to utilize basic maps, diagrams and numerical data in a way that supports the discussion;
- some familiarity with major perspectives in the social sciences;
- some familiarity with relevant social scientific vocabulary.

The main section of an introductory essay is also likely to be moving towards demonstrating:

- an understanding that different theories are in competition:
- the ability to outline the main similarities and differences between these;
- a basic ability to evaluate their strengths and weaknesses.

Conclusions are likely to demonstrate:

- the ability to summarize the content of the essay clearly and concisely and to come to a conclusion.

Quotations should be referenced, and 'pass' essays will always need to avoid plagiarism. Essays should 'flow' smoothly, use sentences, paragraphs and grammar correctly, and be written in clear English.

The 'intermediate' essay

In addition to skills in all the above areas, successful intermediate essays may also show the following.

Introductions are likely to demonstrate:

- a clear understanding of more complex essay questions;
- a basic ability to 'signpost' the content as well as the shape or structure of the essay, but not in a laboured way;
- a grasp of the major debates that lie 'behind the question';
- an ability to define key terms.

Main sections are likely to demonstrate some or all of the following, depending on what the question requires:

- the ability to construct more complex arguments relevant to the question;
- the ability to 'weight' different aspects of the material according to their significance within the overall argument;
- an ability to identify and précis the key debates relevant to the question;
- the ability to outline more complex theories in a basic form;
- an ability to relate abstract ideas and theories to concrete detail;
- an ability to support arguments with appropriate evidence and examples;
- an ability to utilize information drawn from across a wide range of source materials;
- the ability to evaluate critically, that is, identify the strengths and weaknesses of competing positions and make a reasoned choice between these;
- an ability to utilize more complex maps, diagrams and numerical data;
- a preliminary ability to work from original texts and data without relying on commentaries on these;
- increased familiarity with major social scientific perspectives and social scientific vocabulary, and increased confidence in applying these to specific issues;
- a preliminary ability to write from 'within' specific perspectives or theories;
- an ability to pull together different aspects of the course and to apply these to the essay;
- a basic ability in selecting and using appropriate quotations from, and making references to, key texts in the field.

Conclusions are likely to demonstrate:

- an ability to highlight the essay's core argument;
- the ability to provide a basic summary of the key debates raised by the question and the ability to provide an overview of 'current knowledge';
- a preliminary ability to point to absences in the argument or areas worthy of future development.

Essays should also be properly referenced, be written in the author's own words, and utilize a more developed and fluent writing style (for example, by handling transitions effectively).

The 'advanced' essay

In addition to skills in all of the above areas, successful advanced essays may also show the following.

Introductions are likely to demonstrate:

- the ability to present a more sophisticated or nuanced version of the essay's core argument;
- the ability to summarize in more sophisticated forms the key debates raised by the question;
- the ability to provide more sophisticated definitions of terms;
- an ability to interrogate the question by focusing on ideas or sub-questions prompted by the question in hand.

Main sections are likely to demonstrate some or all of the following:

- the ability to construct complex arguments, 'weighting' each section according to its significance within the overall argument;
- the ability to provide sophisticated outlines of complex theories;
- the ability to support arguments with appropriate evidence and examples drawn from a wide range of sources, and to use evidence selectively in a way that supports central points;
- the ability to synthesize and evaluate competing positions critically and the confidence to write from 'within' a specific perspective or theory on the basis of a reasoned understanding of its strengths and weaknesses;
- where appropriate, recognition of the potential uncertainty, ambiguity and limits of knowledge in the field under discussion;
- familiarity with, and confidence in, handling complex maps, diagrams and numerical data;
- familiarity with, and confidence in, handling original texts and data without relying on commentaries;
- familiarity with the major social scientific perspectives and social scientific vocabulary, and confidence in applying these to specific issues and to new contexts;
- the ability to pull together different aspects of the course and apply these to the issues raised by a specific essay question;
- the ability to use appropriate quotations and cite key texts in the field.

Conclusions are likely to demonstrate:

- the ability to present a sophisticated summary of the essay's core argument(s);
- the ability to provide an effective synthesis of the key debates raised by the question, or a sophisticated overview of the state of 'current knowledge';
- a developed ability to point to absences in the argument or areas worthy of future development.

'Advanced' essays should be fully referenced and written in your own words. The best essays are likely to show a significant depth of understanding of the issues raised by the question and may show a more creative or original approach (within the constraints of academic rigour).

Different skills, same writer

In thinking about the requirements of different levels of essay writing, it is important to realize that different levels of skills do not come neatly packaged. For instance, you may already have advanced essay writing skills even while working at an introductory level of undergraduate study. Alternatively, you may have advanced skills of analysis (such as the ability to break down a complex argument into its component parts and summarize these effectively), but be struggling with the handling of theoretical concepts and perspectives. Or you may be very effective at your essay introductions, but shakier when it comes to putting the argument together in the main section. The important point to grasp is that the foregoing advice provides *indications* of what may be expected at different levels across the whole range of abilities, but it is *not* saying that you must be able to demonstrate the appropriate level of ability in all cases. Remember, too, that an essay is always greater than its component parts; it is how you put all those parts together that is often as important as the parts themselves.

You might like to look again at the Essays in Chapter 13. Can you identify some of the criteria above that led Essays 1 and 3 to receive higher marks, and Essays 2 and 4 to receive lower marks? On the basis of the criteria above, and what you have read elsewhere in this guide, are there clues as to whether the essays are written for beginning, intermediate or advanced courses? Are there other challenges you might set yourself as a reader or writer to check your understanding of the interplay between structure, content and style in deciding a grade for a particular essay?

Summary

- Essays are graded on the extent to which they demonstrate an understanding of relevant source material, and of social scientific and writing skills.
- The exact mix of content and skills required will depend on the course and question. However, it is possible to specify in general terms what is expected for each grade band.
- As you become increasingly experienced, you should expect your understanding of social scientific arguments and your writing skills to increase in sophistication.

Self-test

1 What are some of the indicators of an excellent essay? How is this different at introductory and advanced levels of study?
2 What errors will you need to avoid if you want your essay to receive a 'pass' rather than a 'fail'?
3 For you personally, what are the potential problems that you can try to avoid when writing your next essay? What do you think are your particular strengths?

13

Examples of Student Essays

- Essay 1: 'School is a significant site in which sex/gender is produced'. Discuss. (2,000 words)
- Essay 2: 'School is a significant site in which sex/gender is produced'. Discuss. (2,000 words)
- Essay 3: Evaluate the claim that we are now living in an information society. (1,500 words)
- Essay 4: Evaluate the claim that we are now living in an information society. (1,500 words)

If you haven't already done so, read through the following examples of student essays. Essays 1 and 2 are written on the same topic; Essays 3 and 4 are written on another topic.

Essay 1 illustrates how applying the basic standards we have been discussing really can help to produce a good essay. It is a strong essay displaying more advanced writing skills. Depending on the exact requirements of the module, it would probably receive a grade at the top of the range. In contrast, Essay 2 is a weaker essay suggesting less developed social scientific writing skills. Although it might gain a pass mark, it would probably be towards the bottom of the grade range. The word limit for Essays 1 and 2 is 2,000 words.

Essay 3, like Essay 1, is also a strong essay but one written for an early, intermediate module. The Essay 3 question doesn't require the critical sophistication or nuance of Essay 1's, as you would expect from a lower level module, but it does expect some evaluation, achieved through a 'compare and contrast' approach. Essay 3 would probably receive a mark in the higher grade bands, depending on the specific requirements of the module. You will see that Essay 4, while answering aspects of the question, doesn't demonstrate the theoretical depth or evaluative skills of Essay 3. It would, however, probably gain a pass mark, but at the lower end of the grade band. The word limit for Essays 3 and 4 is 1,500 words.

Essay 1

'School is a significant site in which sex/gender is produced.' Discuss

This essay critically explores the claim that school is a significant site in which sex/gender is produced. The claim derives from a broadly social constructionist position, namely one that views sex/gender as being the product of social meanings and practices rather than something biologically given. The essay begins by outlining the social constructionist critique of the biological account of sex/gender. It then reviews recent research on gender and schooling to explore the extent to which the social meanings and practices that make up life in school may be seen as producing relational forms of masculinity and femininity. In exploring these issues, the essay endorses a broadly social constructionist standpoint on gender and schooling, although it also seeks to highlight a number of potential limitations to this position, particularly as these relate to the literature's account of the body and social agency.

Conventional or 'common sense' accounts tend to view masculinity and femininity as biological categories characterized by a range of fixed physical and psychological differences in which the supposed attributes of masculinity (for example, rationality and the capacity for physical action) are valued over those of femininity (for example, intuition and the capacity for caring). The feminist cultural theorist Chris Weedon (1999) locates the origins of these ideas (at least in their contemporary form) in nineteenth-century biological theory and in Victorian middle-class values. However, she also points out that they have been reinvigorated in more recent work in the fields of sociobiology and evolutionary psychology (see for example, Thornhill and Palmer, 2000; Wilson, 1978).

The social constructionist position takes issue with this biologically reductive account. Drawing, in particular, on the work of Michel Foucault (1977, 1984), commentators from this perspective have sought to argue that masculinity and femininity cannot be understood as fixed biological categories but are instead produced in and through social meanings and practices. This position is distinct from earlier sociological accounts of 'sex role' (see for example, Rossi, 1985). Earlier accounts had tended to view gender as the social elaboration of an underlying biological sex difference. Social constructionist theory, on the other hand, argues that the notion of biological sex difference is itself a social construct. For example, Thomas Lacquer (1990) has demonstrated that the notion of distinct male and female bodies arose in the nineteenth century. Prior to this, maleness and femaleness were seen as variations on a single body. Equally, Judith Butler (1993, 2004) has argued that sex/gender is a 'performative enactment'. She suggests that, like other categories of the person, maleness and femaleness do not precede social meanings and practices but are brought into existence through an active 'gendering', that is the citation of sex/gender 'norms' embodied in what, following Foucault, she refers to as discursive practices. Importantly, Butler (1993, p. 238) also argues that gender is systematically (though not inevitably) produced through a 'heterosexual matrix' which equates 'proper forms of masculinity and femininity with heterosexuality and identifies gay masculinities and lesbian femininities as, in some way, 'failed' or 'damaged'.

Bob Connell's influential work in the sociology of masculinity endorses this critique of biological essentialism but questions whether it risks writing the body out of existence. Connell suggests that forms of masculinity and femininity cannot be reduced to supposed biological differences but argues that bodies have 'forms of recalcitrance to social symbolism and control' (see, in particular, Connell, 1995, p. 56).

Connell also suggests that Butler's 'hard' social constructionist account risks writing social agency out of existence. Connell argues that there are multiple versions of masculinity (and, by implication, femininity) that are actively produced through relations of similarity to and difference from key social others. For example, forms of 'laddish', heterosexual, white working-class masculinity may be defined in opposition to forms of 'respectable' middle-class masculinity, to non-white ethnicities, to forms of femininity and to gay masculinities. This argument places a greater emphasis than does Butler's on the notion of pupils as 'active makers of their own sex/gender identities' (Mac an Ghaill, 1994, p. 90). Thus, whereas Butler tends to downplay agency (the active 'speaking' of sex/gender) in favour of a notion of performativity (being 'spoken by' social meanings and practices), Connell retains a stronger account of it.

Drawing on the work of the Italian Marxist Antonio Gramsci (1971), Connell also argues that masculinities and femininities can be understood as being engaged in 'hegemonic struggle'. This refers to an ongoing and potentially shifting process of competition, negotiation, alliance-building and sometimes coercion whereby, under particular conditions, particular versions of masculinity and femininity come to be 'culturally exalted' or 'idealized' while other versions are marginalized and subordinated (see Connell, 1990, p. 83).

Broadly social constructionist ideas of this kind have informed a body of recent literature on sex/gender and schooling (see for example, Duncan, 1999; Epstein and Johnson, 1998; Kehily, 2002; Mac an Ghaill, 1994; Martino and Meyenn, 2001; Martino and Pallotta-Chiarolli, 2003; Skelton and Francis, 2003; Thorne, 1993).

Within this literature, schools are seen as significant sites in which sex/gender is actively produced. This is to say that sex/gender is viewed not as something that is simply brought into the school ready formed but as something actively produced and reproduced in the processes and practices of schooling itself. This active production of sex/gender has a number of dimensions and the following discussion focuses on three of these: the ways in which the content and practices of schooling encode sex/gender; the ways in which pupils actively use sex/gender to negotiate schooling; and the ways in which sex/gender intersects with other social relations.

Perhaps the most obvious means by which sex/gender is said to be produced in the social constructionist literature is via the content and practices of schooling itself. For example, Thorne's (1993) study of two US elementary schools draws attention to the ways in which the categorization of children by gender is threaded through the material and social fabric of the school, such as in teachers' talk ('There's three girls need to get busy', p. 34) or the organization and management of learning (for instance, dividing pupils into gender-based 'teams', p. 67). Similarly, Epstein and Johnson (1994, p. 214) point to the ways in which the regulation of pupils' clothing (in particular, sanctions against girls' clothing thought to connote too overt a sexuality) frequently embodies notions of 'appropriate' or 'proper' forms of gender. While Thorne (1993, pp. 35–6) draws attention to the fact that many aspects of schooling will also play down or contradict gender categorizations, it remains the case that the content and practices of schooling encode sex/gender as a significant category of difference.

However, while sex/gender can be said to be encoded in the content and practices of schooling, the literature also suggests that pupils are themselves active agents in its production. Thorne (1993), for example, describes the children in her study as engaging in 'borderwork', practices by which they actively produce, strengthen and assert sex/gender differences. For instance, she describes a game of team handball which began as a co-operative and informal activity in which gender was not strongly marked but which rapidly accelerated into a more aggressive interaction themed as 'the boys against the girls' (p. 65). In this moment, Thorne suggests, sex/gender was being actively produced (or in Butler's terms, 'performatively enacted') as a significant category of difference.

As well as producing sex/gender through friendship group interactions, the literature also suggests that pupils use sex/gender to negotiate and resist schooling. Kehily and Nayak (1996, p. 214) describe an account from a group of secondary school pupils in which one of them (Samantha) was claimed to have pursued a teacher (Mr Smedley) round the classroom with a sprig of mistletoe with the intention of 'getting some lipstick on the top of his head'. In this instance, a heterosexualized form of femininity is used satirically to undermine the authority of a male teacher (see also Walkerdine, 1981).

While heterosexualized forms of sex/gender are clearly deployed to subvert adult authority, it is also possible to argue that sex/gender is used to negotiate schooling in more subtle ways. For instance, Connell has argued that boys use masculinity to negotiate or build a 'subjective orientation' to the curriculum and that, in the process, the curriculum is important in producing differentiated forms of masculinity. He writes:

> the differentiation of masculinities occurs in relation to a school curriculum that organizes knowledge hierarchically, and sorts students into an academic hierarchy. By institutionalizing academic failure via competitive grading and streaming, the school forces differentiation on the boys. . . . Social power in terms of access to higher education, entry to professions, command of communication, is being delivered by the school system to boys who are academic 'successes'. The reaction of the 'failed' is likely to be a claim to other sources of power, even other definitions of masculinity. Sporting prowess, physical aggression, sexual conquest, may do. (Connell, 1993, p. 95)

This general argument informs Máirtín Mac an Ghaill's (1994) study of a multi-ethnic English secondary school. Mac an Ghaill identifies a variety of differentiated masculinities – the 'macho lads', the 'academic achievers', the 'new enterprisers', and the 'real Englishmen' – through which boys in the school collectively negotiated the curriculum, their home backgrounds and their perceived employment futures. The 'new enterprisers' were, perhaps, particularly interesting in that they broke with the conventional distinction (identified by Connell, above) between anti-academic, 'laddish' forms of masculinity, and pro-school masculinities validated by academic success. Mac an Ghaill argues that the 'new enterprisers' were able to build a pro-school masculine identification out of a newly vocationalized curriculum that offered recognition for academic success in non-traditional subject areas, especially Information and Communication Technologies.

The final area highlighted by the social constructionist literature as a means by which sex/gender is produced in the school concerns the ways in which masculinities and femininities are produced in and through relations of similarity to and difference from social others. As discussed above, Thorne's (1993) concept of 'borderwork' draws our attention to the ways in which sex/gender is used by pupils to produce themselves in gender-differentiated terms. This opposition between forms of masculinity and femininity is perhaps the most central relation underpinning pupils' sex/gender identifications in the school. However, both Mac an Ghaill (1994) and Epstein and Johnson (1998) underline the extent to which school-based masculinities and femininities are also produced in and through relations of age, class, ethnicity and sexuality, as well as in relation to forms of masculinity and femininity deemed subordinate or otherwise inferior.

For instance, Epstein and Johnson cite an exchange between a group of four Muslim girls in a large single-sex comprehensive in which a fifth girl is described in the following terms:

Shamira is not traditional (i.e. she does not occupy a conservative form of Muslim ethnicity). She is a big tart and wears lipstick that doesn't suit her and she walks around sticking her tits out. (Epstein and Johnson, 1998, p. 117)

The girls in this example can be seen to be constructing their own femininity in opposition to Shamira, whose femininity is deemed inappropriately westernized and sexualized. This, then, is an example where sex/gender is spoken through intra-ethnic identifications (traditional versus westernized) and through an opposition to a subordinated femininity (the 'madonna' versus the 'whore'). As Epstein and Johnson also argue, although drawing on wider social relations, such gender constructions occur within and are specific to the dynamics of individual schools.

The girls' appraisal of Shamira in terms of sexuality underlines the centrality of sex and sexuality to the production and policing of gender in pupils' cultures. Mac an Ghaill (1994, pp. 90–6), for instance, describes the ways in which the secondary school boys in his study worked at producing masculinity through 'competitive and compulsive' sexualized talk and practice within their friendship groups. This consisted of the sexual-objectification of girls and women and the homophobic harassment of boys perceived as gay or 'insufficiently masculine'. Epstein and Johnson (1998, p. 158) suggest that anti-lesbian harassment appears less central to girls' culture than does anti-gay harassment to boys' culture. Nevertheless, as the Shamira example demonstrates, they argue that heterosexualized appraisal of other girls is central to the production of femininity within girls' friendship groups.

The recent social constructionist literature has, therefore, made a systematic case in support of the proposition that schooling is a significant site in which sex/gender is produced. It argues that the content and practices of schooling encode sex/gender; that pupils actively use gender to negotiate schooling; and that gender is produced within local pupils' cultures through relations of similarity to and difference from key social others. Work on the relationship between gender and sexuality in the context of the school has been particularly significant. Such arguments, I would argue, fundamentally undermine biologically determinist readings of sex/gender. Nevertheless, it may be possible to qualify the social constructionist account. In particular, following Connell, it is possible to argue that the theoretical tension between a 'hard' social constructionist account (in which social agency is replaced by a notion of performativity) and the emphasis in the literature on pupils as 'active makers of sex gender identities' is not fully addressed or resolved. Equally, it may also be possible to argue that the literature does not fully resolve the exact status of the body in the social constructionist account. However, it remains the case that the recent literature on gender and schooling significantly adds to our understanding of the social construction of gender and sexuality.

References

Butler, J. (1993) *Bodies That Matter*, London, Routledge.

Butler, J. (2004) *Undoing Gender*, London, Routledge.

Connell, R.W. (1990) 'An iron man: the body and some contradictions of hegemonic masculinity', in Messner, M.A. and Sabo, D.F. (eds), *Sport, Men and the Gender Order: Critical Feminist Perspectives*, Champaign, IL, Human Kinetics.

Connell, R.W. (1993) 'Cool guys, swots and wimps: the interplay of masculinity and education', in Angus, L. (ed.), *Education, Inequality and Social Identity*, London, Falmer Press.

Connell, R.W. (1995) *Masculinities*, Cambridge, Polity Press.

Duncan, N. (1999) *Sexual Bullying: Gender Conflict and Pupil Culture in Secondary Schools*, London: Routledge.

Epstein, D. and Johnson, R. (1994) 'On the straight and the narrow: the heterosexual presumption, homophobias and schools', in Epstein, D. (ed.), *Challenging Lesbian and Gay Inequalities in Education*, Buckingham, Open University Press.

Epstein, D. and Johnson, R. (1998) *Schooling Sexualities*, Buckingham, Open University Press.

Foucault, M. (1977) *Discipline and Punish: The Birth of the Prison*, Harmondsworth, Penguin.

Foucault, M. (1984) *The History of Sexuality, Vol. 1: An Introduction*, Harmondsworth, Penguin/Peregrine.

Gramsci, A. (1971) *Selections from the Prison Notebooks*, London, Lawrence and Wishart.

Kehily, M.J. (2002) *Sexuality, Gender and Schooling: Shifting Agendas in Social Learning*, London, Routledge.

Kehily, M.J. and Nayak, A. (1996) 'The Christmas kiss: sexuality, storytelling and schooling', *Curriculum Studies*, vol. 4, no. 2, pp. 211–28.

Lacquer, T.W. (1990) *Making Sex: Body and Gender from the Greeks to Freud*, Cambridge, MA, Harvard University Press.

Mac an Ghaill, M. (1994) *The Making of Men: Masculinities, Sexualities and Schooling*, Buckingham, Open University Press.

Martino, W. and Meyenn, B. (eds) (2001) *What About the Boys?: Issues of Masculinity in Schools*, Buckingham, Open University Press.

Martino, W. and Pallotta-Chiarolli, M. (eds) (2003) *So What's a Boy: Addressing Issues of Masculinity and Schooling*, Buckingham, Open University Press.

Rossi, A.S. (1985) 'Gender and parenthood', in Rossi, A.S. (ed.), *Gender and the Life Course*, New York, Aldine.

Skelton, C. and Francis, B. (eds) (2003) *Boys and Girls in the Primary Classroom*, Buckingham: Open University Press.

Thorne, B. (1993) *Gender Play: Girls and Boys in School*, Buckingham, Open University Press.

Thornhill, R. and Palmer, C.T. (2000) *A Natural History of Rape: Biological Bases of Sexual Coercion*, Cambridge, MA, MIT Press.

Walkerdine, V. (1981) 'Sex, power and pedagogy', *Screen Education*, no. 38, pp. 14–24.

Weedon, C. (1999) *Feminism, Theory and the Politics of Difference*, Oxford, Blackwell.

Wilson, E.O. (1978) *On Human Nature*, Cambridge, MA, Harvard University Press.

Commentary on Essay 1

In reviewing this essay we are not particularly concerned as to whether the answer is 'right' or not. The literature it draws on is from cultural studies and sociology and it is undoubtedly the case that the question of sex/gender could have been addressed from a number of alternative disciplinary points of view – for example, developmental psychology or biology – that might have generated different arguments. Instead, the issue of interest to us is the extent to which the answer demonstrates effective social scientific writing skills. As with any piece of work, the essay is not without flaws. For instance, it could be argued that evidence in support of the 'conventional' view of gender is not explored systematically enough to be rejected with such certainty by the author (although this may simply reflect the balance of argument in the literature the author was required to read). Equally, it could be argued that the concept of sex/gender 'performativity' is not fully explained and that it is not fully illustrated through the research evidence cited. Similarly, the critique of the literature on schooling and sex/gender in the conclusion (the arguments about the status of the body and social agency) appear to repeat Connell's theoretical points without really growing out of the evidence explored in the main section of the essay.

Having said this, the essay has a number of strengths that suggest it should receive a grade towards the top end of the range. Let's explore these in terms of structure and writing skills, content and social scientific skills.

Structure and writing skills

- The essay begins with an introduction that identifies the subject of the essay, indicates the debate lying 'behind' the question, signposts its content and establishes the author's position. (See Section 7.1.)
- The main section uses a standard 'evaluative' structure, that is, it outlines competing positions then explores the evidence for and against them before coming to a conclusion. (See Section 4.3.)
- It builds a logically progressing argument that develops through the following steps: the social constructionist argument is more convincing than the conventional biological account; this is because sex/gender is 'performative' and relational; this can be demonstrated in relation to schooling. (See Section 8.1.)
- It 'flows' reasonably smoothly, is well signposted throughout (see paragraphs 1 and 7), makes use of summary/introductory points (for example, in the

statement, 'As well as producing sex/gender through friendship group interactions, the literature also suggests that . . .') and makes accurate use of spelling, grammar, paragraphing and sentence structure. (See Section 8.4.)

- It provides an evaluative conclusion that summarizes the preceding argument, provides a clear endorsement of the statement in the question, and identifies potential absences in the argument. (See Chapter 9.)
- It is slightly long (2,200 words) but is probably just on the outer limits of acceptability. (As with other regulations, remember to check the rules on essay length that apply to the actual course you are studying.) (See Section 2.3.)

Content

Effective coverage of theoretical issues and research evidence is clearly central to any essay answer. The author of this essay appears to have used or referenced a range of relevant sources and provided detailed coverage of both theoretical material and research evidence. Without knowing the exact content of the course she or he was studying it is difficult to comment on this in much detail, but the coverage looks thorough and the detailed handling of the material suggests wide-ranging reading and a good understanding of the issues.

Social scientific skills

- The answer addresses the question set. (See Section 4.2.)
- The essay is effectively referenced, including page details where necessary. (See Chapter 10.)
- It makes good use of relevant quotations. The Connell quotation is a 'classic' statement of the social constructionist position. The quotation from Epstein and Johnson adds some 'colour' to the argument and is effective in illustrating and illuminating a complex argument. Both support rather than replace points made by the author. (See Section 8.3.)
- Within the confines of a 2,000-word essay, it provides a complex and thorough engagement with relevant theory and applies this theory to and supports it with empirical evidence. (See Sections 2.2 and 8.2.)
- The essay demonstrates effective skills of selection and summary. (See Section 8.2.)
- It provides an effective evaluation of relevant concepts, debates and evidence. (See Sections 2.2, 4.2 and 8.2.)
- It comes to a clear conclusion that is supported by the preceding argument. (See Chapter 9.)
- It makes good use of appropriate academic vocabulary and concepts. (See Sections 8.2 and 8.4.)

Now let's take a look at Essay 2.

Essay 2

'School is a significant site in which sex/gender is produced.' Discuss

This essay looks at the arguments for and against the idea that school is a significant site in which gender is produced. The first section shows where this idea comes from and contrasts it to the deterministic account. The second section gives evidence in favour of the theory of Social Constructionism.

We are used to thinking that gender is biological. Men are men and women are women and this is natural. Sociobiologists and evolutionary psychologists would agree with this point of view. This is called 'Deterministic'. Men are better at rational tasks and thinking in three dimensions. They are also stronger. Women are better at intuition thinking and emotionality. E.O. Wilson is an example of this approach. However, writers such as Foucolt, Butler and Connell have challenged this. They argue that gender is constructed in practices and meanings, such as the 'enactment of gender norms'. Butler calls this 'performativity'.

Connell argues that gender is hegemonic'. This means that there are different types of masculinity in competition but that certain types (such as sportsmen) are 'idealized' (Connell, 1990). Connell got this idea from Gramsci, an Italian Marxist. An example of hegemonic masculinity is given by Swain who argues that playing football in the playground makes boys dominant in the school because this draws on a sporting version of masculinity that is dominant in the wider society (Swain, 2000).

Foucolt is very important in this Social Constructionist theory. He argued that the term 'homosexual' does not refer to a pre-existing identity but constructs that identity. This does not mean that same-sex sexual activity did not happen before the nineteenth century (when the term homosexual was invented), it means that that same-sex sexual activity did not imply a particular type of personality (the homosexual) before this. The homosexual is therefore Socially Constructed as of course is the heterosexual. Butler argues that biological sex is also a Social Construction (Butler, 1993).

Schools are a place where Social Construction happens. This has been argued by many eminent Academic thinkers including Mac an Ghaill and Epstein. Connell argues that masculinities appear in relation to the curriculum.

the differentiation of masculinities occurs in relation to a school curriculum that organizes knowledge hierarchically, and sorts students into an academic hierarchy. By institutionalizing academic failure via competitive grading and streaming, the school forces differentiation on the boys. . . . Social power in terms of access to higher education, entry to professions, command of communication, is being delivered by the school system to boys who are academic 'successes'. The reaction of the 'failed' is likely to be a claim to other sources of power, even other definitions of masculinity. Sporting prowess, physical aggression, sexual conquest, may do. (Connell, 1993)

This is one way that schools Socially Construct gender.

A second way is that children actively produce gender for themselves. Take the example of children lining up to leave the classroom. They used to be told to form lines so that girls were in one line and boys were in another. In fact, I remember that in my first school it still had two entrances one marked for boys and the other for girls. Foucolt would see this as an example of the ways in which schools produce sexual difference. Now however girls and boys will be told to form a single line but Barry Thorne argues they will still try to form lines according to gender.

This is an example of boys and girls actively producing gender for themselves which Thorn calls 'borderwork' (Thorn, 1993).

Sexuality is a big theme in much of this writing on schooling and gender. There are lots of examples where children use sexuality to try to undermine there teachers. A famous one is Valerie Walkerdines example of two little boys calling their nursery teacher rude names. Many people are surprised that children as young as this would dare to be so cheeky. Another example is the 'Christmas kiss' story told by Kehily and Nayak (1996). In this case a secondary school girl chased her male teacher round the classroom with a sprig of mistletoe and claimed she was trying to kiss him on the head. The pupils liked to retell this story so that the story itself was one way in which they 'had a laff' and resisted the authority of the school. Unfortunately the teacher had a nervous breakdown. These examples also show how gender is used in the classroom to 'negotiate the curriculum' indicating how schools Socially Construct gender.

Mac an Ghaill (1994) is very interested in the ways in which boys use homophobic abuse to police other boys. To be identified as a sissy is to invite homophobic abuse whether or not on defines oneself as gay, often in the form of more or less ritualized humour. The use of humour and insult constitutes a regulatory practice by young men in schools through which they establish and exhibit heterosexual masculinities. The forms humour and insult employed are primarily either sexist (for example, the teasing and harassment of girls or insult to other boys via insulting their mothers or sisters) or homophobic abuse of young men who did not display 'hyper-masculinity'. Swain talks about this too. He describes how the football-playing boys in his research would abuse boys who weren't very good at football by calling them 'Gaylord' and 'poofter'. Since these boys were at primary school calling them homosexual was not because they were homosexual but because this was a way of saying they were like girls. The point Swain is making is that football is a dominant form of masculinity in our society and that the boys in the school tried to lay claim to dominance in there own right by being good at football. However, this dominance was also at the expense of other social groups such as girls, homosexuality and boys who weren't any good at football. Mac an Ghaill argues that boys 'make up' collective identities as boys out of a Compulsory Heterosexuality, Misogyny and Homophobia.

> heterosexual male students were involved in a double relationship, of traducing the 'other', including women and gays (external relations), at the same time as expelling femininity and homosexuality from within themselves (internal relations). (Man an Ghaill, p. 90)

Barry Thorne describes how one boy in her research was called a 'sissy' by other boys because he wore a one-piece snow suit which they thought was 'wimpy' and because he liked to play girl's games in the playground as well as playing boys games. She says he was a bit of a loner and didn't have many friends. Some children were more likely to get away with this sort of thing. A girl got away with it because she was a good athlete and because she could fight which gave her respect with the other children. But one of the teachers described her as 'wanting to be a boy'.

There are three ways that schools produce gender. The pupils produce gender for themselves. The school produces gender through things like making children line up in different lines. And the children 'negotiate the curriculum'.

In conclusion, this has essay has presented a lot of evidence to show that 'school is a significant site in which gender is produced'. In fact, Christine Heward describes schools as 'masculinity factories' and I would tend to agree with her. Gender is obviously very important in the school day. Schools are always doing things that reproduce gender even though they sometimes try to do the opposite of this. And even when schools do try do the opposite of this the children themselves resist this by reproducing conventional ideas about gender (Thorne). Butler calls this 'performativity' but you could see it from the 'Deterministic' point of view of which EO Wilson is an example which would argue that the children are just being boys and girls because they are programmed to be this way by Evolution. This argument is difficult to get away from at the end of the day because there are some obvious differences between men and women so we probably should expect to see these in children as well. I would argue that we need to have a Middle Ground where we put together the Deterministic and the Social Constructionist point of views. In fact, this is what Connell argues when he says that you cant get away from the body.

The body, I would conclude is inescapable (Connell)

This is what I would argue.

References

Butler, J. (1993) 'Bodies That Matter'.

Connell, R.W. (1995) *Masculinities*, Polity Press.

Epstein, D. and Johnson, R. (1998) *Schooling Sexualities*, Buckingham: Open University Press.

Foucault (1977) *Discipline and Punish: The Birth of the Prison*,

Kehily, M.J. and Nayak, A. (1996) *'The Christmas kiss: Sexuality, storytelling and schooling'*, Curriculum Studies.

Mac an Ghaill, M. (1994) 'The Making of Men: Masculinities, Sexualities and Schooling', Buckingham: Open University Press.

Swain, J. (2000) 'The money's good, the fame's good, the girls are good: the role of playground football in the construction of young boys' masculinity in a junior school', *British Journal of Sociology of Education*, 21, 1: 95–109.

Commentary on Essay 2

You can probably see for yourself that this essay is not as strong an answer to the question as that provided by Essay 1. Why is this? Again, we can break down our thoughts into issues related to structure and writing skills, content and social scientific skills.

Structure and writing skills

Although the essay has an introduction, conclusion and some signposting, its structure and the writing skills displayed are weak. In particular:

- The introduction is underdeveloped compared to Essay 1. It does not establish the author's position on the question and both the signposting and the allusion to the debate lying 'behind' the question are vague. (See Section 7.1.)
- There are systematic errors in spelling and punctuation (e.g. 'there' instead of 'their'; incorrect use of the apostrophe; unnecessary use of capital letters on terms such as 'social constructionism'), sentences are sometimes cumbersome and paragraphs are sometimes too short. (See Section 11.4.)
- There are errors in the spelling of several authors' names (Foucolt instead of Foucault; Barry Thorne instead of Barrie Thorne).
- The brief section beginning, 'To be identified as a sissy is to invite homophobic abuse . . .', and ending, 'homophobic abuse of young men who did not display "hyper-masculinity"', is plagiarized from Epstein and Johnson (1998, p. 181). (See Section 11.5.)
- Although the essay begins by discussing theory and then moves on to look at empirical evidence, the logical progression of the argument is problematic. For

instance, the relevance of paragraph 5 to the question needs to be more clearly established, while the material on sexuality and schooling is not clearly located as an example of the ways in which gender is produced in schooling practices. (See Section 8.1.)

- Given the word limit, the essay is rather short (1,500 words). (Remember to check the rules on essay length that apply to the actual course you are studying.)

Content

The material covered appears to be relevant to the question set, drawing on similar literature to Essay 1. However, the understanding of this material appears to be much shallower in comparison to that displayed in Essay 1 and the breadth of detailed reading (as evidenced in the identification of major arguments and relevant evidence) appears more limited.

Social scientific skills

Once again, these areas are weak compared to Essay 1.

- Referencing is inconsistent and incomplete. (See Chapter 10.)
- The introduction and conclusion are thin. (See Chapters 7 and 9.)
- Handling of theory is poor, suggesting an inadequate understanding of the material. For example, although the discussion of Foucault and homosexuality is good, the concepts of performativity and hegemony are not fully explained. (See Sections 2.2 and 8.2.)
- Both the Mac an Ghaill quotation and the first Connell quotation are used without a full explanation of the points being made. (See Section 8.3.)
- The empirical evidence is sometimes left to 'speak for itself' without a full explanation of the point it is being used to illustrate or support. (See Section 8.2.)
- The information cited about the author's own schooldays detracts from the professionalism of the argument by appearing merely anecdotal. (See Section 11.3.)
- The evaluative conclusion is undermined by an incorrect understanding of Connell's argument about the relationship between the body and the social.
- Use of appropriate academic vocabulary is underdeveloped. (See Section 8.2.)

Essays 3 and 4 address a different question but again demonstrate the ways in which good academic practice can produce a stronger essay.

Essay 3

Evaluate the claim that we are now living in an information society

It has been claimed that the vast development of technology in recent years has changed the way we live, that we now live in an 'information society'. We no longer rely on agriculture or manufacturing to fuel the economy; it is knowledge and information that is at the economic core. The availability of information is facilitated by new communications technologies, which some see as revolutionizing society. This essay will consider the arguments of Manuel Castells, who posits the information society as the revolutionary organizational structure of contemporary society, involving changes in the uses of time and space (Hamilton, 2002, p. 113). It will also offer an alternative argument from Peter Golding who considers the information and communication technologies of today as continuities with the past, along with relevant historical evidence. Finally the essay will evaluate the presented debates and evidence and assess the relevance for our understanding of contemporary society.

Manuel Castells identifies changes in the use of time and space – from agrarian time relying on nature to the onset of industrialization with factories and regulatory clock-time – that, he argues, are key aspects of social change. The move now is towards 'timeless time', which involves less rigidity and increased flexibility, a veritable annihilation and de-sequencing of time. Instantaneous communication and global transactions are possible; life-cycle timings are becoming indistinctive, for example reproduction and life expectancy (Lury, 2002, p. 151). Castells suggests that this is made possible by the development of information and communication technologies (ICTs), indeed he claims these technologies are as revolutionary as those of the industrial era. This information age, according to Castells, is organized by a 'network society' (cited in Hamilton, 2002, p. 123).

For Castells the information/network society is a new and revolutionary social form. Whilst he sees this as dominated by ICTs he does recognize other contributing factors, such as the restructuring of capitalism, the collapse of communism and the increase of social movements, such as feminism and environmentalism. (Hamilton, 2002, p. 113). This is in line with the notion that social changes co-exist and are multiple. (Jordan and Pile, 2002, p. xiv).

One significant area of social change is the increasing influence of globalization, which links closely with the information society and networks theory. Castells sees networks as interconnecting nodes across geographical locations, used to an immediate advantage but disposed of when no longer beneficial. This is opposed to former, centralized, hierarchical forms of organization (Bashforth et al., 2004, p. 72). According to Castells these networks and ICTs have had such a significant impact on the reordering of time and space that a new societal form has emerged.

Castells argues that ICTs enable simultaneous and instant actions without physical contiguity. Purchases made by telephone, or global transactions occur in what he terms the 'space of flows'. The space of flows has contributed to the emergence of 'timeless time', which according to Castells is a '. . . relentless effort to annihilate time' (quoted in Hamilton, 2002, p. 126). Time is compressed and de-sequenced, for example, shopping via the internet at anytime. This aspect of societal change is acknowledged positively by some. Negroponte sees that the availability of ICTs and access to knowledge can have an equalling effect on society (cited in Hamilton, 2002, p. 111). However, Castells also notes negative consequences on societal inequalities, in particular, the power of the knowledge providers and those excluded through lack of access to the technologies, leading to a polarized society. (Mackay, 2002, p. 143).

Castells also observes the impact of technology on a cultural level. The technology available within the home no longer flows one-way. Communication technologies facilitate interactivity and a wide range of information is streamed into the home, creating diversity and agency. These seemingly extensive changes are shown to impact society on a micro-level within the private sphere of the home. This, according to Castells and Thompson, is a characteristic of modernity (Mackay, 2002, p. 144).

Whilst Castells claims this new society is revolutionary, Peter Golding argues that these technologies are just a progression of what has passed before, allowing increased speed and efficiency: he classes these as 'technology one'. What Golding sees as revolutionary are the bio and nanotechnologies, classed as 'technology two' (Hamilton, 2002, p. 129). Golding cites the significance of the telegraph in Victorian society. The telegraph challenged boundaries of time and space in ways never experienced before. Technology journalist, Tom Standage, (1998) comments that, '. . . it was the Victorians, not today's internet generation that experienced most fully the shrinking of time and space' (quoted in Mackay, 2002, p. 152). Golding therefore refutes the claim that contemporary ICTs are revolutionary.

Golding also questions the claim of the information society's theory of the compression of time and space. He draws attention to the increase of traffic congestion and air travel. He notes that the majority of travel is functional rather than leisure orientated (Hamilton, 2002, p. 132–133). Golding perceives the reordering of time and space as a feature of modernity, identified by Giddens as 'time-space distanciation'. This refers to the stretching of relations over distances of time and space, for example, the long distance telephone call. Golding considers this an aspect of modernity, rather than a revolutionary effect of ICTs.

In questioning the claim that we live in an information society, Golding refutes the notion that ICTs will be available and beneficial to all. Negroponte claims that inequalities will be generational rather than class based. However, Golding cites evidence confirming the social division of internet access, with higher income groups being the high users. Golding points out that ICTs need constant updating, thus incurring continuing costs and inhibiting availability to lower income groups, and thus distinguishing social groups. This reinforces societal structures of inequalities (Hamilton, 2002, p. 130). This is also a key aspect of Bourdieu's theory of cultural capital (Savage, 2002, p. 77).

Golding also observes inequalities within the employment sector. He disputes claims that work has been revolutionized by noting the increase of working hours. Alongside this, and despite the growth of the ICT sector, unemployment rates are higher now than in previous generations. Low paid sectors of IT work exist, with mainly female employees, thus reinforcing gender inequalities (Hamilton, 2002, p. 130). Golding sees this as continuities persisting. As Keohane and Nye (1998) remark with regards to theories of new societies, '. . . overlook how much the new world rests on the traditional world . . .' (quoted in Hamilton, 2002, p. 130). This raises the question of just how new is the structure of the acclaimed information society?

Having presented the competing theories from Castells and Golding on the information society this essay will evaluate their claims and account for their relevance in today's society, beginning with Castells' revolutionary claim of a new information and network society. A revolutionary claim implies a sudden event resulting in a new social form (Hamilton, 2002, p. 119). However, Castells' logic is flawed as he himself acknowledges that ICTs have developed gradually. His theory lacks empirical adequacy as he overlooks the significance of past history, as in the case of the telegraph. Whereas Golding, by contrast, offers a more coherent framework by acknowledging the significant impact of the telegraph on society. (Mackay, 2002, p. 152).

Castells' argument also seems contradictory at points. He observes emerging societal inequalities induced by ICTs; the dominance and power of the knowledge providers – and the exclusions. Yet the theory focuses on the transformation of society through the use of ICTs. This suggests that the theory is not comprehensive enough to cover all aspects of society (Mackay, 2002, p. 143). In contrast, Golding provides quantitative evidence of inequalities with regards to ICT usage – and demonstrates the continuity of structural inequalities. This position is supported by a Marxist and Weberian perspective. The Marxist stance views ICTs as a progression of a capitalist structure. Weberians see it as rationalization of society – or increasing regulation of the people (Hamilton, 2002, p. 104).

A key feature of Castells' theory is the reordering of time and space. Castells assumes that this change is solely due to ICTs. Although compression and de-sequencing of time is partly due to ICTs, it is also an aspect of modernity. Furthermore, Hamilton highlights the fact that society is still mostly, '. . . time-bound, place-bound worlds' (Hamilton, 2002, p. 115). This is evident in Silva's study of everyday routines showing daily life is organized through patterns and routines of time (Silva et al., 2002, p. 284). Even Castells notes that his networks require a material infrastructure, suggesting a further lack of coherence in his theory. (Hamilton, 2002, p. 126).

Perhaps a major critique of Castells' framework is the exaggeration of the impact of ICTs in today's society. Alternatively, Golding perhaps underestimates the progression of ICTs. His understanding that the need for social interaction and the tangible experience of shopping being the reasons for the early lack of popularity of internet shopping seems somewhat naïve, when mail-order shopping had been a feature of society for many years (Hamilton, 2002, p. 132), although he does comment that with technological advances this may change. Likewise, Mackay (2002, p. 162) acknowledges the unpredictable future of technologies.

This essay has aimed to present debates regarding the claim that we live in an information society, from Castells' revolutionary claims of the impact of ICTs transforming social structures to Golding's argument that society is undergoing constant change and progression. It seems that Castell's claims are over-optimistic and ambitious. Whereas Golding's argument more coherently explains today's society, with his acknowledgment of increasing social divides and the seeming tendency of ICTs to inadvertently reinforce inequalities. Golding observes that aspects of society progress through constant change, which is multi-faceted, co-existing and consists of multiple changes (Jordan and Pile, 2002, p. xiv). Therefore, it is reasonable to accept Golding's position that today's society is not a new information society, but one of progression and continuity.

(Word count: 1598)

References

Bashforth, H., Bennett, T., Braham., Doak, R., Hamilton, P., Jewkes, Y., Parr, J., Redman, P., Sherratt, N. and Thompson, K. (2004) *Sociology and Society, Study Guide*, Milton Keynes, The Open University.

Braham, P. and Janes, L. (Eds) (2002) *Social Differences and Divisions*, Oxford, Blackwell/Milton Keynes, The Open University.

Hamilton, P. (2002) 'From industrial to information society', in Jordan, T. and Pile, S. (Eds) (2002) *Social Change*, Oxford, Blackwell/Milton Keynes, The Open University.

Hemmings, S., Silva, E. B. and Thompson, K. (2002) 'Accounting for the everyday', in Bennett, T. and Watson, D. (Eds) (2002) *Understanding Everyday Life*, Oxford, Blackwell/Milton Keynes, The Open University.

Jordan, T. and Pile, S. (2002) 'Social change: introduction', in Jordan, T. and Pile, S. (Eds) (2002) *Social Change*, Oxford, Blackwell/Milton Keynes, The Open University.

Lury, C. (2002) 'Everyday life and the economy', in Bennett,T. and Watson, D. (Eds) (2002) *Understanding Everyday Life*, Oxford, Blackwell/Milton Keynes, The Open University.

Mackay, H. (2002) 'New media and time-space reconfiguration', in Jordan, T. and Pile, S. (Eds) (2002) *Social Change*, Oxford, Blackwell/Milton Keynes, The Open University.

Savage, M. (2002) 'Social exclusion and class analysis', in Braham, P. and Janes, L. (Eds), *Social Differences and Divisions*, Oxford, Blackwell/Milton Keynes, The Open University.

Commentary on Essay 3

As with the first two essays, we are less concerned with whether the answer is 'right'. The concept of the information society remains a contested one, so our interest is in whether the essay compares well the two main theorists introduced on this module, Castells and Golding, using a social scientific approach. While there are flaws in this essay, you will probably recognize that it is a strong answer in many regards.

Structure and writing skills

- The introduction begins with the oft-repeated claim about the 'information society', effectively rehearsing the title of the essay, but in the student's own words. It signals the key debates (revolution versus continuity) and theorists (Castells and Golding) to be cited, and clearly signposts the sequence of the discussion. (See Chapter 7.)
- The main section uses a compare and contrast approach, with Castells, the author of *The Network Society* and therefore its main proponent in the essay, given primary attention. (See Sections 4.3 and 8.1.)
- In the first part of the main body, different concepts illuminating Castells' argument are rehearsed. Some of the complexities – and inconsistencies – of Castells' arguments are acknowledged, but the general point that we are living in a 'new', 'revolutionary' network society, facilitated by ICTs, remains central. (See Sections 6.1 and 8.2.)
- In the second part of the main body, Golding's contrasting position is explored in some depth. In addition, some of Golding's (and others') empirical evidence is presented. (See Section 8.2.)
- The third part of the main body evaluates Castells' and (to a lesser extent) Golding's claims by using some of the basic tools of social science evaluation: evidence, coherence, comprehensiveness. (See Section 6.1.)
- The conclusion summarizes the main discussions, the flaws in Castells' claim, and concludes that, on balance, there is stronger evidence for 'continuity' than for 'revolution'. (See Sections 6.1 and Chapter 9.)
- The word count, set at 1,500 words, is within a 10 per cent allowance. (See Section 2.3.)
- The spelling, grammar and punctuation is generally all good, though there are a couple of incomplete sentences, e.g. 'From Castells' revolutionary claims of

the impact of ICTs transforming social structures to Golding's argument that society is undergoing constant change and progression.' (See Section 11.4.)
- The logic of the essay is good and the flow is okay, though at points the essay feels a bit like a 'list' of Castells' key concepts. This is, however, a promising attempt at building a discussion sequence, if not fully realized. (See Section 8.1.)
- The reference list is well set-out and broadly follows the Harvard style. (See Chapter 10.)

Content

On this module, it is acceptable to use only the set texts and consequently all of the references are from these. On a more advanced course it would probably be required to read Castells in the original and the tutor might expect a longer set of 'outside' references. Castells' arguments are generally well drawn, as are the criticisms of his claims, from Golding and others. There is also an attempt to synthesize the meta-theories of Marx and Weber, and Bourdieu, although in each case a clearer discussion of why their thinking was particularly helpful would have strengthened the essay.

Now, there is potentially a serious problem with the essay – one might argue that it doesn't really answer the question. An obvious approach to the question would have been to consider in greater detail the evidence that our lives remain predominantly concerned with our immediate environments and face-to-face relations and that these still happen primarily in 'real time'. Further evidence might have included employment in the service sector – which includes call centres, but also includes hairdressers, shop assistants and other personal and professional services. This might have been set in contrast to the claims and evidence provided by Castells. However, this student chose to prioritize the theoretical debates informing our notion of the information society – and the question of whether this is indeed something 'new' – and within the context of the module, this was appropriate.

Social scientific skills

This is a real strength of this essay.

- The essay addresses the question, albeit in a non-obvious fashion, in appropriate depth given the short word count. (See Sections 2.3 and 4.1)
- The citations are close to perfect, though in a few cases Giddens' ideas are represented as Silva's (when in fact Silva was reporting Giddens' arguments). (See Section 8.3.)
- There is a good selection of quotes, though these are not integrated into the essay in a particularly fluid way. They do, however, illuminate the argument. (See Section 8.3.)

- The student deployed both theory and empirical evidence (both quantitative and qualitative) and made a suitable attempt to evaluate both using tools of critical analysis – discussing, for instance, whether Castells' argument was coherent. (See Sections 6.1, 8.2 and 8.3.)
- If you look carefully through the essay, you will see that the student effectively works through the circuit of knowledge in her discussion of the 'claim'. (See Section 2.2.)
- There is a strong use of key concepts which are generally defined correctly. (See Section 8.3.)
- The evaluation is clear and the judgement 'sound', based on the evidence provided and the argument developed through the essay. (See Sections 6.1, 6.2 and 8.2.)

Essay 4

Evaluate the claim that we are now living in an information society

The information society is all around us: we are surrounded by technology that influences every aspect of our lives. We go to bed listening to the radio and wake up and watch TV, we talk with our friends on the phone and play computer games in our leisure time. In the West, our economy is dependent on technology and socially we could not live without it. This is very different to the past when people didn't have technology and society and the economy were organized differently.

In agrarian societies, people were dependent on the sun to wake them up and they only worked when there was light. The patterns of work were determined by the seasons and the harvest. People were mostly very poor and lived in a subsistence economy, which means they only produced enough food to live on, and didn't trade for better goods. Because of this, they also only really knew the people that lived close by and there was a lot of competition for food, water and shelter.

Nowadays, according to Marx, we live in a capitalist society. There are those who own the means of production and those who only own their own labor. They are, respectively, the capitalist class and the proletariat. Capitalism emerged at the same time as the industrial revolution. The industrial revolution meant that people no longer woke with the sun, but were dependent on the factory clock for telling them when to work and how long for. As people left the land, they became urbanized and accustomed to working shifts and the electric light meant that people could work longer hours. All of this labor and capital investment made for a surplus of goods which could then be sold for a profit, making the capitalists richer. But it also meant that we could buy more things and as industrialism progressed and the factory systems became more efficient (Taylorism) we could buy them cheaper; so in a capitalist economy everyone benefits. People were also able to socialize more because they were living in cities. Vaudeville was popular and then the invention of cinema meant that people could join in great crowds to enjoy modern culture together.

Now, however, products are available globally. We live in a time of globalization. According to Castells, time and space have been annihilated (Hamilton, p. 126). For instance, call centre workers in India can support IT users in the US, which means that there is IT support 24 hours a day. This is good because it means that we never have to be without our computers and the economy can keep going 24/7. Also, because of automation, we can shop whenever we like on the internet. Security is less of a problem nowadays because of the encryption of data on secure websites. In fact ICTs have changed the way that we live beyond all recognition. Castells, according to Hamilton, talks about the concept 'space of flows' which is when the geographical location of people is irrelevant, but because of telephones and computers, transactions can still happen instantaneously even though we are not face to face in the same geographical location. We can also keep in touch with friends and family abroad. Email and Facebook are good examples of this. A more extreme example is 'World of Warcraft' where people can be friends and play against each other, even if they have never met – and, because of living in different parts of the world, never will.

Castells says we live in a 'network society' (the title of one of his books), which means that things are no longer organized from a central point, but may be diffuse and connected by nodes. According to Negroponte, this is a good thing. If things aren't centralized, or hierarchical, there is a chance they can be shared on the ground-level. In other words, the network society is more egalitarian – we have an equal shot at getting information and knowledge, which are the key drivers of the information society. An example of this is Wikipedia which ensures that everyone can have access to the same information – and if they have specialist knowledge they can add it to the pool.

In agrarian societies and even in the early periods of industrialization it was difficult to share knowledge and information, partly because most people couldn't read, but also because there was no way of linking people together beyond their immediate communities. So, while the industrial revolution was a revolution, the information society is even more of a revolution, according to Castells.

Castells says that 'timeless time' (Hamiliton, p. 126) and the 'space of flows' mean that we are living in a new type of society and that this is a major break from the old society. We are still a capitalist society and Castells is a Marxist who recognizes this, but what gets traded isn't so much food, but more money, investments and information. Money is no longer 'real' but is just represented and traded electronically, as though it were. Some people now live their entire lives on-line. For instance, last year a woman became the first Second Life millionaire by selling accessories for your avatar in her Second Life store (The Guardian). She has an avatar, a store and products, none of which are real, but gets actual money through PayPal for her products. This way of working and living is revolutionary.

However, not everyone agrees with Castells. Golding, for instance, says that the information society is just a later version of modern capitalism. All the ICT technologies have done is speed things up and made them more efficient (Taylorism). For Golding, the real revolution is yet to come and will be driven by bio and nanotechnologies which will change us biologically (Hamilton, p. 129). Social change is also just a progression of the changes that occurred with urbanization and the factory system. He gives evidence that the wealthy will continue to increase their wealth because they can afford the new technologies, leading to a 'digital divide'. Unlike Castells, Golding suggests that this divide will be between nations and between individuals in nations and that egalitarianism is unlikely. In fact, he says that people are working longer hours at less satisfying jobs and that call centres are just factories by another name. They are mindless and soulless and people are driven to work in them for very low wages because there is a surplus of labor (Marx). There is a surplus of labor because new technologies are more efficient (the hours worked in the home have reduced because 'white goods' and other labor-saving devices have meant less time is spent cleaning, etc.). There is also a surplus because workers can live anywhere, and capitalists can shop around different countries for the cheapest labor.

Critics such as Frank Webster argue that:

> contemporary society first of all is still a capitalist society oriented towards accumulating economic, political, and cultural capital. They acknowledge that information society theories stress some important new qualities of society (notably globalization and informatization), but charge that they fail to show that these are attributes of overall capitalist structures. Critics such as Webster insist on the continuities that characterise change. In this way Webster distinguishes between different epochs of capitalism: laissez-faire capitalism of the 19th century, *corporate capitalism* in the 20th century, and informational capitalism for the 21st century. (Wikipedia, 2010, http://en.wikipedia.org/wiki/Information_society, accessed 26 August 2010).

However, all this is only possible because of new technologies. Castells is right to say that information and knowledge are the defining features of contemporary society and our economy. Without computers, I would be unable to write this essay, or research it and I wouldn't be able to keep up contact with my friends. In the future, I am likely to work in an industry that is completely reliant on new technologies. We live in an information society. This is completely different from agrarian societies where you only knew and worked with the people close by. It is also very different from early industrial societies because we are not dependent on the clock or the location of the factory for our work – we can live anywhere and still be employed. Castells is right.

(Word count: 1361)

References

Bennett, T. and Watson, D. (Eds) (2002) *Understanding Everyday Life*, Oxford, Blackwell/Milton Keynes, The Open University.

Castells, M. (1996) *The Rise of the Network Society*, Oxford, Blackwell.

Hamilton, P. (2002) 'From industrial to information society', in Jordan, T. and Pile, S. (Eds) (2002) *Social Change*, Oxford, Blackwell/Milton Keynes, The Open University.

Jordan, T. and Pile, S. (Eds) (2002) *Social Change*, Oxford, Blackwell/Milton Keynes, The Open University.

Mackay, H. (2002) 'New media and time-space reconfiguration', in Jordan, T. and Pile, S. (Eds) (2002) *Social Change*, Oxford, Blackwell/Milton Keynes, The Open University.

Marx, K. and Engels, F. (1888) *The Communist Manifesto*.

Savage, M. (2002) 'Social exclusion and class analysis', in Braham, P. and Janes, L. (Eds), *Social Differences and Divisions*, Oxford, Blackwell/Milton Keynes, The Open University.

Wikipedia (2010) 'Manuel Castells' and 'Information Society', http://en.wikipedia.org/wiki/Information_society (accessed 26 August 2010).

Commentary on Essay 4

You will probably notice that Essay 4 has a structure that is recognizably inspired by the question, in particular the content word 'now'. However, it is a weaker essay than Essay 3 for reasons to do with its writing, content and social science skills. This is not to say it is without merit – it is quite enjoyable to read, and there are sections that work well, but it is not a *good* social science essay.

Structure and writing skills

The essay has an introduction, a conclusion and some recognizable structure to the main body. However, signposting is limited and the essay relies on colloquial expressions rather than clear and consistent academic prose.

- The introduction makes a claim that is in accord with the question, but doesn't introduce the possibility that this claim might be contested, nor does it suggest how this might be evaluated. What it does do is indicate that the contemporary period marks a break from the past, suggesting that a historical approach will be taken. (See Chapter 7.)

- The main body is organized to consider 'earlier' historical periods – agrarian society and the early period of industrialization – and then to consider whether 'society' and the 'economy' are organized differently today. (See Section 8.1.)
- Although most of the sentences make sense, there is less coherence to the paragraphs, with many lacking a topic sentence, containing tangential material, or concluding on an unrelated point. (See Section 8.4.)
- There is no signposting of the direction of the essay, nor are there transition words or phrases to help guide the reader. (See Sections 7.1 and 8.4.)
- Towards the end of the essay, criticisms of Castells' position are introduced, but not developed – and they are summarily dismissed in the conclusion. (See Chapter 6.)
- The essay question expressly asks for evaluation, but there is little evidence of this. Most of the essay is descriptive. (See Sections 2.3, 4.2 and 4.3.)
- The writing is quite engaging and lively, but the colloquialisms are a distraction. (See Section 8.4.)
- The large (and only) quotation is not integrated with the rest of the essay and seems to be doing most of the work of presenting a counter-claim to Castells. It is also lifted directly from Wikipedia (though it is referenced). (See Section 5.3, 8.3 and 10.2.)
- The conclusion restates the introduction and also introduces new illustrations ('Without computers, I would be unable to write this essay'; 'In the future, I am likely to work in an industry that is completely reliant on new technologies'). It also makes the bold statement that 'Castells is right', but doesn't draw effectively on the discussion in the main body of the essay to justify this conclusion. (See Chapter 9.)
- In addition, the sudden shift to the first- and second-person singular in the conclusion undermines the academic authority of the essay. (See Section 8.4.)
- The word count is a little low, but within the 10 per cent range of 1,500 words. (See Section 2.3.)

Content

There is relevance to the set question, but the essay focuses almost exclusively on addressing the content word 'now', rather than on the contested 'claim' that we are living in an 'information society'. Despite the process word 'evaluate', much of the essay is descriptive. As the question is from a second level module, it is probably expected that the essay would compare and contrast, as well as evaluate, different theoretical positions. In this case, only Castells' theory of the information society is explored in any depth and even this is largely peripheral to the description of the changes in social activity and the economy. The empirical evidence cited is largely unreferenced and anecdotal. It is not clear that the student understands some of Castells' key concepts, for instance 'timeless time', though it is certainly helpful to have attempted to use them. There are far fewer references than in Essay 3, and many of them are vague (e.g. 'Taylorism', 'Marx'). The lack of references, inconsistent use of key concepts, inadequate discussion and evaluation, anecdotal 'evidence', etc. make this a much shallower essay than Essay 3.

Social scientific skills

- Given that the student has chosen to take a historical approach, there is surprisingly little exploration of possible *continuities* with the past, nor is there a consideration of contemporary agrarian societies/labor. Contextualization of the discussion is poor. (See Sections 2.2, 4.3 and 6.1.)
- The use of theory is very thin and one-sided. The essay would be more appropriate to an advocacy question, but as evaluation is required, at least one contrasting theory to Castells' claim needs to be adequately explored. (See Section 4.3.)
- Contradictions in the discussion go unnoticed, for instance, the student claims that money is no longer 'real', but then uses the example of the Second Life millionaire who has earned 'actual money' from her Second Life store. (See Section 6.1.)
- Social scientific tools are not in evidence: there is no interrogation of the 'claim', no weighing up of empirical evidence, and what evidence is cited is poorly referenced and largely anecdotal, etc. There are also innumerable unsubstantiated claims and assumptions about agrarian and early industrial societies. (See Sections 2.2, 6.1, 8.2 and 8.3.)
- Referencing is incomplete and the use of Wikipedia is unhelpful. In addition, the student claims to have read Manuel Castells' *The Rise of the Network Society* (see References list), but there is no evidence in the essay that she has done so. (See Section 5.3 and Chapter 10.)

Summary

- The material in this chapter illustrates stronger and weaker student essays.
- The strengths and weaknesses relate to: writing skills (such as the use of paragraphs and transitions); the structure of the argument; content; and social scientific skills (such as the use of theory and evidence).
- Analysing the essays will help you identify what constitutes effective social scientific essay writing.

Self-test

1 What techniques of 'critical reading' might you use when reading the four student essays?
2 What elements of structure, content and style have you identified as being better/worse in each of the essays?
3 What is missing from each of the essays? (Answer: administrative requirements such as name, title page, etc.)

Appendix A: Abbreviations and Words in Foreign Languages

At various points in your reading, especially in references, you will come across various abbreviations or words written in foreign languages. You may need to use these in your own writing, so here's a list of some of the more common examples.

cf. *(confer)*	compare
ch., chs (or chap., chaps)	chapter(s)
ed., eds	editor(s)
edn	edition
e.g. *(exempli gratia)*	'for example' (not to be confused with 'i.e.'). Used when an actual example is given, as in the following: 'Some forms of analysis (e.g. Marxist and feminist theories) suggest that social phenomena are the product of underlying and prior social divisions.'
et al. *(et alii)*	'and others', used for multiple authors as in '(Hatt et al., 1978)'
et seq. *(et sequens)*	'and the following' (for example, pp. 16 *et seq.*)
etc. *(et cetera)*	'and the rest'/'and so on'
ff. *(folio)*	alternative to *et seq.* (for example, pp. 16 ff.)
ibid. *(ibidem)*	'in the same work' (as the last reference). Used in footnotes/endnotes to save writing out the whole reference again (for example, 'Ibid. p. 61')
i.e. *(id est)*	'that is' (not to be confused with 'e.g.'). Used to explain, define or clarify as in the following: 'Radical feminists (i.e. feminists who maintain that gender relations are the product of a universal and unitary system of male dominance) argue that ...'
loc. cit. *(loco citato)*	'in the same place' (as the previous passage)
n., nn.	note(s), as in 'p. 4, n. 2'

op. cit. *(opere citato)*	'in the work recently cited' as in 'Gilroy, op. cit., p. 67'; used in footnotes/endnotes to save writing a full reference for a work previously cited, but not the last reference (cf. 'ibid.')
p., pp.	page, pages
passim	throughout the work (not on one page only)
q.v. *(quod vide)*	'which see' (for cross-referencing)
(sic)	'thus'; indicates that questionable/apparently incorrect quoted material is faithfully reproduced from the original
trans., tr.	translator
vol., vols	volume(s)

Appendix B:
Editors' Symbols – Common
Notations Made by Tutors

Ex.? or e.g.?	Include an example or illustration.
Gr.	Grammar is faulty.
Ref. or cit.	A reference is required.
Run-on	The sentence amalgamates too many topics, or is actually two (or more) thoughts or sentences run together.
Incompl.	The sentence is incomplete – it may lack a verb or subject, or some other essential element. May also be used to indicate an incomplete argument or essay.
Punc.	Punctuation is faulty.
Sp.	Spelling is incorrect.
w/c	Word choice. Indicates that the tutor is not sure you have said what you mean – or perhaps thinks you have misunderstood a term. Suggests there is a more appropriate or accurate word.
✓	Can mean: 'I have read this bit', 'Good' or 'Correct' – you may wish to clarify this with your tutor.
✗	Incorrect.
⅄	Insert here. Often used when there is a note in the margin. This symbol indicates where in the text an additional or replacement word, phrase, example, etc. might be inserted.
≈	Approximately the same, but not quite. Can be used when an example doesn't actually support an argument, or when a translation of an argument isn't quite right.
≠	Not the same.
¶	Requires a new paragraph.
~~Your words~~	A line through your words could mean that they are superfluous to the sentence or paragraph, or that they are incorrect. If you are not sure, ask your tutor.
Words your	The wavy line suggests swapping the words, sentence or paragraph around, in this case to read 'Your words'.

References

Andrews, G. (2005) 'Dissent and the re-invention of politics', in Andrews, G. and Saward, M. (eds), *Living Political Ideas*, Edinburgh, Edinburgh University Press/The Open University.

BPS (1994) *Guidelines for External Examiners on Undergraduate Psychology Degrees*, Leicester, British Psychological Society/Association of Heads of Psychology Departments.

Burns, T. and Sinfield, S. (2008) *Essential Study Skills: The Complete Guide to Success at University*, 2nd edn, London, Sage.

Coats, M. (undated) *Open Teaching Toolkit: Learning How to Learn*, Milton Keynes, The Open University.

Cogswell, D. (2007) *Chomsky for Beginners*, Danbury, Connecticut, For Beginners LLC.

Cole, S. and Harris, P. (undated) *Open Teaching Toolkit: Revision and Examinations*, Milton Keynes, The Open University.

Hart, C. (2001) *Doing a Literature Search: A Comprehensive Guide for the Social Sciences*, London, Sage.

Iyengar, S. (2010) 'On the Art of Choosing', (vodcast) TED Talks, posted July 2010 at www.ted.com/talks/sheena_iyengar_on_the_art_of_choosing.html (Accessed 2 August 2010).

MacKay, H. and Reynolds, P. (2001) 'Social science and making sense of the information society', in MacKay, H., Maples, W. and Reynolds, P., *Social Science in Action: Investigating the Information Society*, Milton Keynes, The Open University.

Moor, L. (2004) 'Brands, property and politics', *Soundings*, 28, Winter, pp. 49–61.

Nash, K. (2009) 'Between citizenship and human rights', in *Sociology*, vol. 43, no. 6, pp. 1067–83.

Office for National Statistics (2009) *Social Trends 39, Labour Force Survey* (online) http://www.statistics.gov.uk/downloads/theme_social/Social_Trends 39/Social_Trends_39.pdf, p. 59 (Accessed 7 July 2010).

Redman, P. (2002) 'Writing in your own words', Milton Keynes, The Open University.

Rubin, D. (1983) *Teaching Reading and Study Skills in Content Areas*, London, Holt, Reinhart and Winston.

Seely, J. (2009) *The Oxford A–Z of Grammar and Punctuation*, 2nd edn, Oxford, Oxford University Press.

Sherratt, N., Goldblatt, D., Mackintosh, M. and Woodward, K. (2000) DD100 *An Introduction to the Social Sciences: Understanding Social Change, Workbook 1*, Milton Keynes, The Open University.

Skelton, C. and Francis, B. (2003) 'Introduction: boys and girls in the primary classroom', in Skelton, C. and Francis, B. (eds), *Boys and Girls in the Primary Classroom*, Buckingham, Open University Press.

Taylor, A. (2003) 'Trading with the environment', in Bingham, N., Blowers, A. and Belshaw, C. (eds), *Contested Environments*, Chichester/Milton Keynes, Wiley/The Open University.

The Open University (1994) 'Appendix B: some comments on essay writing', D309 *Cognitive Psychology, Assignments Booklet*, Milton Keynes, The Open University.

The Open University (2010) 'Harvard Guide to Citing References', http://library.open.ac.uk/help/howto/citeref/index.cfm, internal only site (Accessed 10 August 2010).

Truss, L. (2006) *Eats, Shoots and Leaves: The Zero Tolerance Approach to Punctuation*, New York, Gotham.

Urry, J. (2010) 'Consuming the planet to excess', in *Theory, Culture & Society*, vol. 27, nos 2–3, pp. 191–212.

Webb, J. (2009) *Understanding Representation*, London, Sage.

Index

NOTE: Page numbers in *italic type* refer to figures.